wishes™

fall in love with cardmaking

GIBBS SMITH
TO ENRICH AND INSPIRE HUMANKIND
Salt Lake City | Charleston | Santa Fe | Santa Barbara

First Edition
13 12 11 10 09   5 4 3 2 1

Copyright © 2009 JRL Publications

Created by: Jeanette R. Lynton
Executive Director: Kristine Widtfeldt
Creative Manager: Kristy McDonnell
Art Director: Eric Clegg
Project Manager: Stacy San Juan
Editors: JoAnn Jolley, Tori Bahoravitch, Quinn Nielsen
Design: Traci O'Very Covey
Photographer: Skylar Nielsen
Photo Stylist: Suzy Eaton

Thanks to all the talented artists who helped to make these wonderful
cards come to life.

Published by
Gibbs Smith
P.O. Box 667
Layton, Utah 84041

1-800-835-4993 Orders
www.gibbs-smith.com

Gibbs Smith books are printed on either recycled,
100% post-consumer waste, or FSC-certified papers
Printed and bound in China

Library of Congress Control Number: 2008942890
ISBN 13: 978-1-4236-0437-2
ISBN 10: 1-4236 0437 7

Warm wishes, birthday wishes, holiday wishes—nothing says I wish you well quite like a handmade card. It's love in an envelope! A handmade card says something about the giver and communicates something special to the recipient. And now, it's even easier to communicate your fondest wishes in a handmade card, thanks to *Wishes*, an all-new collection of card patterns and inspiring artwork.

my wish for you

With this latest pattern book, I have a wish for each of you: that you'll fall in love with card making all over again.

The patterns are all new and so simple to follow—I adore making the circle cards using the templates included on the CD. And on each page, you'll find fresh techniques using my favorite tool, clear stamps! And of course, you'll find plenty of inspiration in the hundreds of artwork samples featured throughout. Recreate one of my favorite cards, or use the patterns and your own ideas to create an original look all your own. Whether you're looking to create a stack of cards in an afternoon, or one special card that lasts forever, my wish is that you'll find your passion on these pages.

Wishing you many happy hours of crafting beautiful handmade cards!

Jeanette

Jeanette R. Lynton

JEANETTE R. LYNTON

Since the 1970s, Jeanette has enjoyed a passion for preserving treasured memories, and early in life began creating exclusive stamps and sharing her scrapbooking knowledge. Today, Close To My Heart, the company Jeanette founded, is a leader in the scrapbooking and stamping industry, owning many of the categories that dominate the market, including true 12" x 12" scrapbook albums, double-sided background and texture paper, lay-flat page protectors, and clear stamps.

Always at the forefront of innovation and creativity, Jeanette's pioneering products include a series of instruction programs offering simple guidelines for dynamic scrapbooking layouts and inspiring easy-to-make cards. These best-selling books continue to delight and instruct novice and expert crafters alike.

Jeanette's artistic eye and "let me show you how" approach have made scrapbooking faster, simpler, and easier than ever before, while continuing to enhance the art of preserving memories and celebrating relationships.

Make a wish to create more cards, more beautifully, and more simply, then watch it come true with *Wishes*, the newest collection of card patterns from innovator Jeanette R. Lynton. In this fun and fabulous book, you'll find 85 all-new patterns that can be rotated for even greater variety. Plus, you'll find unique tips, techniques, and resources to make your card creations even more spectacular, including:

a template CD for placement-perfect shapes and just-right envelopes, stamping secrets to make each card a sensation, hundreds of artwork options to inspire your creativity, and an exclusive new series designed to help you create many cards from a single cutting diagram. On pages 20, 68, and 110, you'll find these three "mini-workshops" that will help you create multiple themed cards in a flash. Perfect for your next holiday card or invitation!

Whatever you're wishing for in a card program, you'll find it all—and more—in *Wishes*!

· · ·

contents

quick reference

2½" × 3½"

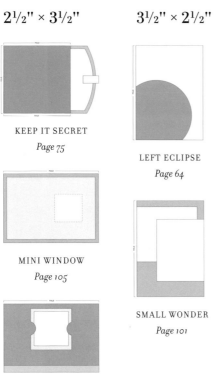

KEEP IT SECRET
Page 75

MINI WINDOW
Page 105

TINY TABS
Page 41

WELL ROUNDED
Page 27

3½" × 2½"

LEFT ECLIPSE
Page 64

SIMPLE STRIP
Page 37

SMALL WONDER
Page 101

THREE IN A ROW
Page 41

3" × 3"

A CUT ABOVE
Page 49

LAYERED LOOK
Page 19

MIDDLE GROUND
Page 19

MINI COMBINATION
Page 84

RIGHT AWAY
Page 84

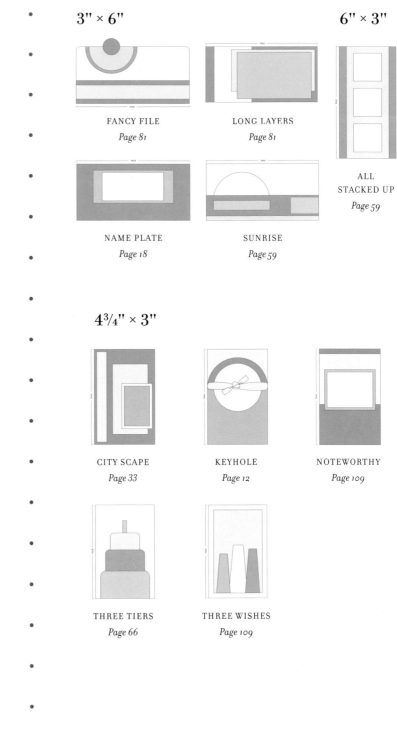

3" × 6"

FANCY FILE
Page 81

LONG LAYERS
Page 81

NAME PLATE
Page 18

SUNRISE
Page 59

6" × 3"

ALL
STACKED UP
Page 59

4¾" × 3"

CITY SCAPE
Page 33

KEYHOLE
Page 12

NOTEWORTHY
Page 109

THREE TIERS
Page 66

THREE WISHES
Page 109

4½" circle

ATTENTION GETTER
Page 46

BOX IT OFF
Page 93

CENTER CIRCLES
Page 117

INNER COURT
Page 67

MERRY-GO-ROUND
Page 30

RICOCHET
Page 127

SIDE NOTE
Page 127

SIMPLE STATEMENT
Page 11

SIMPLY SECURE
Page 46

TIMELESS TRIO
Page 45

4½" × 4½"

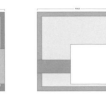

ALL SQUARED UP
Page 101

ALL TUCKED IN
Page 94

CORNER SHOP
Page 39

CURTAIN CALL
Page 94

FANCY FOUR
Page 76

FOLDED FOCUS
Page 56

JUST RIGHT
Page 39

MATCHBOOK
Page 76

UP IN THE CORNER
Page 121

WINDOW WISHES
Page 121

quick reference

$4^1/4" \times 5^1/2"$

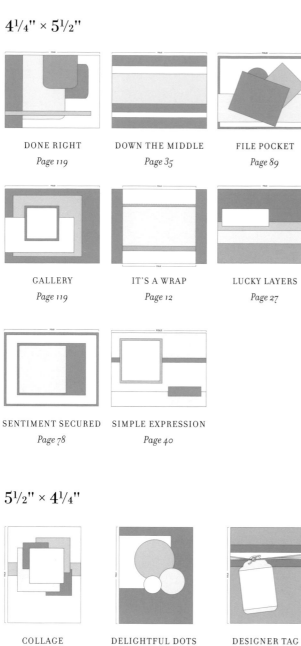

DONE RIGHT
Page 119

DOWN THE MIDDLE
Page 35

FILE POCKET
Page 89

GALLERY
Page 119

IT'S A WRAP
Page 12

LUCKY LAYERS
Page 27

SENTIMENT SECURED
Page 78

SIMPLE EXPRESSION
Page 40

$5^1/2" \times 4^1/4"$

COLLAGE
Page 97

DELIGHTFUL DOTS
Page 53

DESIGNER TAG
Page 97

GEOMETRIC
Page 124

ON THE EDGE
Page 53

STAY LEFT
Page 55

$5^1/2" \times 4^1/4"$ CONTINUED

SUN DIAL
Page 14

$5" \times 7"$

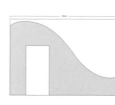

WINDSWEPT
Page 103

$7" \times 5"$

BULLSEYE
Page 33

CIRCLE COLLECTION
Page 29

CONFIDENTIAL
Page 122

CUBED COLLAGE
Page 92

FRAMEWORK
Page 15

MEDALLION
Page 52

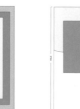

MIDPOINT
Page 77

ON THE BALL
Page 47

SIMPLICITY
Page 106

6" × 6"

DESIGNER TAB

Page 125

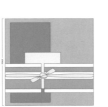

ENCHANTING
ENCLOSURE

Page 31

FAR-SIDED FOCUS

Page 80

KEEP IT LEVEL

Page 107

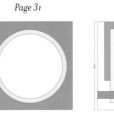

OPEN OUTLINE

Page 98

PIECED TOGETHER

Page 34

SATCHEL

Page 38

3½" × 8"

CLASSIC CLOSURE

Page 62

TOP VIEW

Page 86

8" × 3½"

LOWER LAYERS

Page 57

RIGHT DESIGN

Page 42

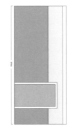

ROUNDABOUT

Page 61

SENTIMENT WAVE

Page 118

SIMPLE SIDE VIEW

Page 83

SIMPLY SAID

Page 17

TOP BAND

Page 100

TOP IT OFF

Page 50

quick reference

celebration

For the pattern to
Framework see page 15.

For the pattern to
Well Rounded (left) see page 27.

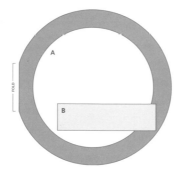

4½" circle

ideas! *For more artwork featuring this pattern see page 67.*

S I M P L E   S T A T E M E N T ™

instructions

1 Using a 4½" circle card (template 1) with the fold on the left side as your base, attach piece A to the center of the card front.

2 Attach piece B to the card front placing it in the bottom right corner as desired.

3 Embellish as desired.

paper dimensions

A 3½" Circle (template 3)
B ¾" × 1¾"

Jeanette's Tip

To give your project just a hint of color, use second generation stamping by stamping once on scrap paper then stamping a second time on your project. The extra touch of color subtly complements your artwork.

Celebrate LOVE.
IT IS THE *breath* OF YOUR EXISTENCE AND
THE BEST OF ALL REASONS *for living.*

instructions

1 Using the Keyhole template provided, trim piece B.

2 Using a 4¾" × 3" card with the fold on the left side as your base, attach piece A to the bottom of the card front, keeping the edges flush.

3 Attach piece B directly above piece A, keeping the straight edges flush.

4 Attach piece C to the card front, placing it ½" from the top and centered from side to side.

5 Wrap ribbon E around the card front; tie a knot and trim ends.

6 Embellish as desired.

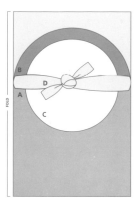

4³/₄" × 3"

paper dimensions

A 3" × 3"
B 2½" × 3"
C 2½" Circle (template 5)
D 9" ribbon

ideas! *For more artwork featuring this pattern see page 51.*

instructions

1 Using the It's a Wrap template provided, trim and fold piece A to form the card base.

2 Attach piece B to the large flap of piece A, keeping the top and side edges flush.

3 Attach piece C to piece B, 1" from the top, keeping the side edges flush.

4 Adhere the top flap of piece A to create a card sleeve. Insert piece D into the card sleeve.

5 Embellish as desired.

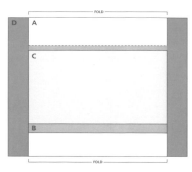

4¼" × 5½"

paper dimensions

A 9½" × 4¼"
B 3½" × 4¼"
C 2¼" × 4¼"
D 4¼" × 5½"

ideas! *For more artwork featuring this pattern see page 61.*

For the pattern to
Curtain Call (right) see page 94.
For the pattern to
Far-Sided Focus (center) see page 80.
For the pattern to
Fancy Four (left) see page 76.

For the pattern to
Curtain Call (right) see page 94.
For the pattern to
Far-Sided Focus (center) see page 80.
For the pattern to
Fancy Four (left) see page 76.

Jeanette's Tip

Add a fun accent to the back of your card by stamping in the corner and layering with embellishments.

instructions

1 Using the Sun Dial template provided, trim piece D.

2 Using a 5½" × 4¼" card with the fold on the left side as your base, attach piece A to the bottom of the card front keeping the edges flush.

3 Attach piece B directly above piece A, keeping the edges flush.

4 Attach piece C to the card front, placing it ⅜" from the top and centered from side to side.

5 Attach piece D to the card front directly above piece B keeping the straight edges flush.

6 Embellish as desired.

paper dimensions

A   1¼" × 4¼"
B   ¾" × 4¼"
C   2" × 3½"
D   1½" × 3"

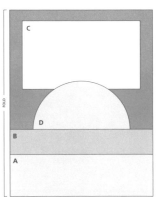

5½" × 4¼"

ideas! *For more artwork featuring this pattern see page 106.*

Jeanette's Tip

When stamping in lighter colors of ink, outline the image with a pen or marker to make it stand out and be more defined.

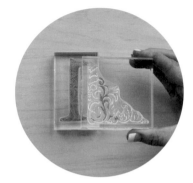

step 1 To create a pattern on an otherwise solid stamp, ink your solid stamp, then lightly touch or "kiss" a second stamp to the inked surface.

step 2 Being careful not to let the stamp slide, gently separate stamps to pull away the ink. Stamp the new patterned image on cardstock.

instructions

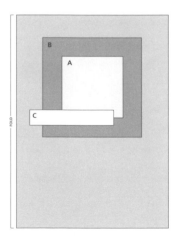

7" × 5"

ideas! *For more artwork featuring this pattern see pages 10 and 120.*

1 Attach piece A to the center of piece B.

2 Using a 7" × 5" card with the fold on the left side as your base, attach piece B to the card front, placing it ¾" from the top and centered from side to side.

3 Attach piece C to the card front, placing it 3¼" from the top and ½" from the left side.

4 Embellish as desired.

paper dimensions

A 2" × 2"
B 3¼" × 3¼"
C ½" × 2¾"

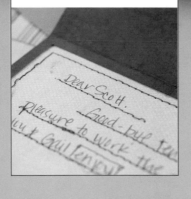

Jeanette's Tip

To personalize the inside of a card, I love using stitched lines for journaling that special message.

For the pattern to Noteworthy (top) see page 109.
For the pattern to Right Design (bottom) see page 42.

THE MORE YOU *praise* AND CELEBRATE YOUR LIFE,

THE MORE THERE IS IN LIFE TO *celebrate.*

—OPRAH WINFREY

step 1 Stamp image on a sticky note or scrap piece of paper and cut out part of image you don't want to stamp on your artwork.

step 2 Place mask on artwork and stamp directly over it. Remove the mask to reveal the desired part of the image on your artwork.

instructions

1 Using an 8" × 3½" card with the fold on the left side as your base, attach piece A to the left side of the card front, keeping the edges flush.

2 Attach piece B directly to the right of piece A, keeping the edges flush.

3 Attach piece C to piece D, centered top to bottom, keeping the left edges flush.

4 Attach piece D to the card front, placing it 1" from the bottom, keeping the left edges flush.

5 Embellish as desired.

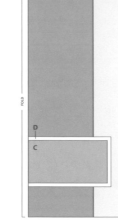

8" × 3½"

ideas! *For more artwork featuring this pattern see page 79.*

paper dimensions

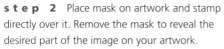

A   8" × 2¼"
B   8" × 1"
C   1½" × 2¾"
D   1¾" × 2⅞"

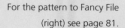

For the pattern to Fancy File
(right) see page 81.

Jeanette's Tip

For a uniquely distressed image, ink your stamp, blot it with a tissue, and then stamp your image.

• • • • N A M E   P L A T E ™ • • • •

instructions

1 Attach piece A to the center of piece B.

2 Using a 3" × 6" card with the fold on the top as your base, attach piece B to the card front, placing it ¼" from the top and centered from side to side.

3 Embellish as desired.

```
                    FOLD
   ┌─────────────────────────────┐
   │  ┌───────────────────────┐   │
   │ B│ A                     │   │
   │  │                       │   │
   │  └───────────────────────┘   │
   └─────────────────────────────┘
```

3" × 6"

paper dimensions

A   1½" × 3¼"
B   1¾" × 4¼"

ideas! *For more artwork featuring this pattern see page 75.*

CELEBRATE THE *happiness* THAT FRIENDS ARE ALWAYS GIVING,
MAKE EVERY DAY A HOLIDAY AND CELEBRATE *just living!*

—AMANDA BRADLEY

MIDDLE GROUND™

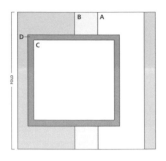

3" × 3"

paper dimensions

A 3" × 1"
B 3 × ½
C 1¾" × 1¾"
D 2" × 2"

ideas! *For more artwork featuring this pattern see pages 40 and 126.*

instructions

1 Using a 3" × 3" card with the fold on the left side as your base, attach piece A to the card front, placing it ¼" from the right edge, keeping the top and bottom flush.

2 Attach piece B directly to the left of piece A, keeping the top and bottom flush.

3 Attach piece C to the center of piece D.

4 Attach piece D to the card front placing it ¼" from the left edge and centered from top to bottom.

5 Embellish as desired.

LAYERED LOOK™

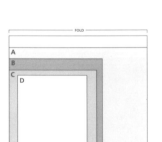

3" × 3"

paper dimensions

A 2¾" × 3"
B 2" × 2¼"
C 1¾" × 2"
D 2" × 1½"

ideas! *For more artwork featuring this pattern see page 43.*

instructions

1 Using a 3" × 3" card with the fold on the top as your base, attach piece A to the bottom of the card front, keeping the edges flush.

2 Attach piece B to the card front, placing it ½" from the top, keeping the left edges flush.

3 Attach piece C to piece B, keeping the bottom and left edges flush.

4 Attach piece D to the card front, placing it ⅛" from the bottom and ¼" from the left edge.

5 Embellish as desired.

Perfect for the everyday celebrations in your life, the Celebration Card Workshop will help you make 12 beautiful handmade cards in a snap (two each of six designs). The 6" × 6" cards are a fun and unique size, which is a smart use of paper for you and something different and memorable for those you give them to. Your friends will love them! And don't forget the envelopes: you'll find a coordinating envelope template on the included CD. To get started, you'll need the following papers:

12" × 12" cardstock (8)
12" × 12" Background and Texture papers (2)

Six pieces of your cardstocks will be used as your card bases, and the remaining two will be cut using the diagrams below. Select two complementary but different patterned papers to give your cards both consistency and variety. Next, simply follow the cutting diagram and the assembly instructions for each card and, in no time at all, you'll have 12 beautiful cards ready to celebrate any occasion! You'll also want to

choose your favorite embellishments—for these samples, simple chocolate ribbon and coordinating brads make just the right impression. And don't forget the sentiments! Stamping words of love, encouragement, thanks and praise will let your friends know just how much they mean to you. You'll have plenty of cardstock left over after you follow the cutting diagrams and it's easy to stamp images on those extra pieces. For a completely different card look, check out the Celebration Card Workshop made with different papers and embellishments, shown on page 25.

CARDSTOCK

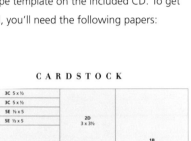

CARDSTOCK

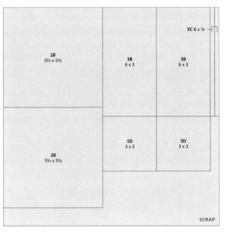

B & T PAPER

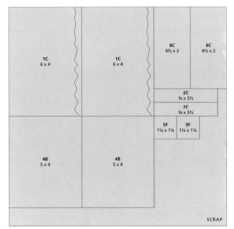

B & T PAPER

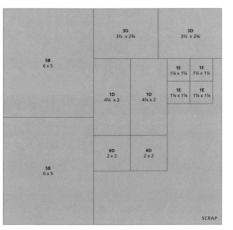

CARDSTOCK (6)*

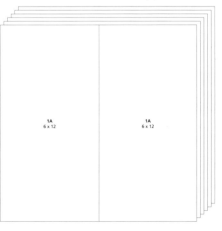

Choose six cardstocks for your card bases, labeling them 1A, 2A, 3A and so forth. Cardstocks may be the same color or coordinating colors, depending on your preference.

instructions

1 Fold piece 1A in half, forming a 6" × 6" card base with the fold on the left.

2 Attach piece 1B to the card front, placing it centered from side to side, keeping the top and bottom flush.

3 Attach piece 1C to the center of piece 1B, keeping the top and bottom flush.

4 Attach piece 1D to the card front, placing it ⅜" from the top and 1½" from the right edge.

5 Attach pieces 1E to piece 1D, placing them ½" from the bottom, centered from side to side and ¼" from each other.

6 Embellish as desired.

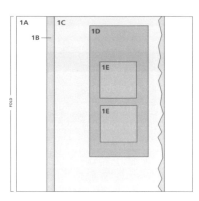

6" × 6"

paper dimensions

1A 6" × 12"
1B 6" × 4"
1C 6" × 4" (torn 6" × 3½")
1D 4¼" × 2"
1E 1¼" × 1¼" (2)

instructions

1 Fold piece 2A in half, forming a 6" × 6" card base with the fold on the left.

2 Attach piece 2B to the card front, placing it ⅜" from the top and left edges.

3 Attach piece 2C to piece 2D, placing it ¼" from the top, keeping the side edges flush.

4 Attach piece 2D to the card front, placing it 2" from the top, keeping the right edges flush.

5 Embellish as desired.

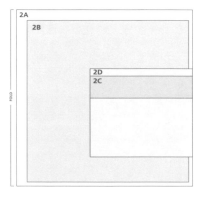

6" × 6"

paper dimensions

2A 6" × 12"
2B 5½" × 5½"
2C ¾" × 3½"
2D 3" × 3½"

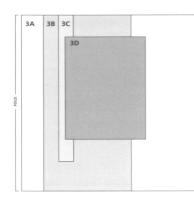

6" × 6"

paper dimensions

3A 6" × 12"
3B 6" × 3"
3C 5" × ½"
3D 3½" × 2¾"

instructions

1 Fold piece 3A in half, forming a 6" × 6" card base with the fold on the left.

2 Attach piece 3B to the card front, placing it ¾" from the left edge, keeping the top and bottom flush.

3 Attach piece 3C to piece 3B, placing it ½" from the left edge, keeping the top flush.

4 Attach piece 3D to the card front, placing it ¾" from the top and 1½" from the left edge.

5 Embellish as desired.

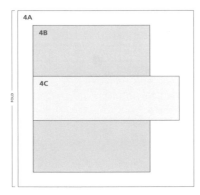

6" × 6"

paper dimensions

4A 6" × 12"
4B 5" × 4"
4C 1½" × 5"

instructions

1 Fold piece 4A in half, forming a 6" × 6" card base with the fold on the left.

2 Attach piece 4B to the card front, placing it ½" from the top and left edge.

3 Attach piece 4C to 4B, placing it 1¾" from the top, keeping the left edges flush.

4 Embellish as desired.

instructions

1 Fold piece 5A in half, forming a 6" × 6" card base with the fold on the left.

2 Attach piece 5B the left side of the card front, keeping the edges flush.

3 Attach piece 5C directly to the right of piece 5B, keeping the edges flush.

4 Attach piece 5D to the card front, placing it ½" front the top and 1" from the left edge.

5 Attach piece 5E to the card front, placing it 1" from the bottom, keeping the left edges flush.

6 Attach piece 5F to piece 5E, placing it ½" from the right edge.

7 Embellish as desired.

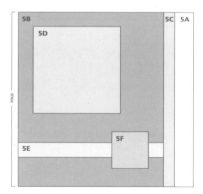

6" × 6"

paper dimensions

5A   6" × 12"
5B   6" × 5"
5C   6" × ¼"
5D   3" × 3"
5E   ½" × 5"
5F   1¼" × 1¼"

instructions

1 Fold piece 6A in half, forming a 6" × 6" card base with the fold on the left.

2 Attach piece 6B to the center of the card front.

3 Attach piece 6C to piece 6B, placing it ¼" from the top and left edges.

4 Attach piece 6D to the card front, placing it 1" from the top and 1¾" from the left edge.

5 Embellish as desired.

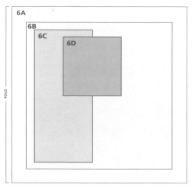

6" × 6"

paper dimensions

6A   6" × 12"
6B   5" × 5"
6C   4½" × 2"
6D   2" × 2"

congratulations

¡felicitaciones!

For the pattern to
Open Outline see page 98.

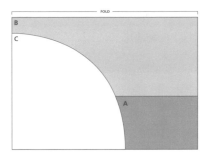

FOLD

2½" × 3½"

paper dimensions

A 1" × 2"
B 1½" × 3½"
C 2¼" × 2½"

i d e a s ! *For more artwork featuring this pattern see pages 11 and 108.*

i n s t r u c t i o n s

1 Using the Well Rounded template provided, trim piece C.

2 Using a 2½" × 3½" card with the fold on the top as your base, attach piece A to the bottom right corner of the card front, keeping the edges flush.

3 Attach piece B to the top of the card, keeping the edges flush.

4 Attach piece C to the bottom left corner of the card front, keeping the straight edges flush.

5 Embellish as desired.

IT'S THE *little* MOMENTS
THAT MAKE *life big.*

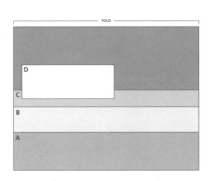

FOLD

4¼" × 5½"

paper dimensions

A 1¼" × 5½"
B ¾" × 5½"
C ½" × 5½"
D 1" × 2¾"

i d e a s ! *For more artwork featuring this pattern see page 117.*

i n s t r u c t i o n s

1 Using a 4¼" × 5½" card with the fold on the top as your base, attach piece A to the bottom of the card, keeping the edges flush.

2 Attach piece B directly above piece A, keeping the edges flush.

3 Attach piece C directly above piece B, keeping the edges flush.

4 Attach piece D to the card front, placing it 1" from the top and ⅜" from the left edge.

5 Embellish as desired.

congratulations

For the pattern to Right Away
(left) see page 84.
For the pattern to Matchbook
(right) see page 76.

Made for Gma—
mom's day 5/5/12

well

done

ideas! *For more artwork featuring this pattern see page 85.*

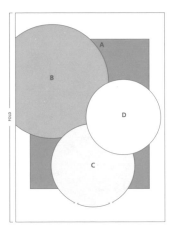

7" × 5"

TIPS & TECHNIQUES
using the front and back of stamps

step 1 Flip over desired stamp and apply to a block so the back side is facing up. Ink and stamp.

step 2 Turn the stamp over, ink, then stamp the design.

instructions

1 Using the Circle Collection template provided, trim piece B.

2 Using a 7" × 5" card with the fold on the left side as your base, attach piece A to the center of the card front.

3 Attach piece B to the card front, placing it ½" from the top, keeping the left edges flush.

4 Attach piece C to the card front, placing it 1" from the right edge and ½" from the bottom.

5 Attach piece D to the card front, placing it ⅛" from the right edge and 2" from the bottom.

6 Embellish as desired.

paper dimensions

A 5" × 4"
B 4¾" × 3¾"
C 2½" Circle (template 5)
D 2" Circle (template 6)

For the pattern to Inner Court
(right) see page 67.

Jeanette's Tip

Make stamping even easier by placing multiple stamps on the same block. This technique works especially well with alphabet stamp sets.

• • • MERRY - GO - ROUND ™ • • •

paper dimensions

A 4" Circle (template 2)

B 3¾" × 1¼"

C 4¾" × ½"

instructions

1 Using the Merry-Go-Round template provided, trim piece B.

2 Using a 4½" circle card (template 1) with the fold on the left side as your base, attach piece A to the center of the card front.

3 Attach piece B to the right of piece A, keeping the right edges flush.

4 Attach piece C directly to the left of piece B. Trim edges.

5 Embellish as desired.

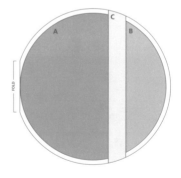

4½" CIRCLE

ideas! *For more artwork featuring this pattern see page 65.*

6" × 6"

ideas! For more artwork featuring this pattern see page 45.

instructions

1 Using a 6" × 6" card with the fold on the left side as your base, attach piece A to the card front, placing it ¼" from the top and left edges.

2 Attach piece B to the card front, placing it 2½" from the top and 1¼" from the left edge.

3 Attach piece C to piece D, placing it ¼" from the top, keeping the side edges flush.

4 Attach piece D to the center of piece E, keeping the side edges flush.

5 Wrap piece E around the card, centering edges on piece B.

6 Wrap ribbon around the card front. Tie a knot centered over piece B and trim ends.

7 Embellish as desired.

TIPS & TECHNIQUES
emboss resist

step 1 Stamp image in embossing ink. Coat with clear embossing powder and heat emboss.

step 2 Using a sponge loaded with colored ink, sponge around image.

paper dimensions

A	5½" × 2¾"
B	2½" × 2½"
C	½" × 11¾"
D	1½" × 11¾"
E	2" × 11¾"
F	15" Ribbon

congratulations

For the pattern to Left Eclipse
(top) see page 108.
For the pattern to Sentiment Wave
(bottom) see page 118.

Fly High!

well done on your new promo

You can do ANYTHING YOU WISH TO DO,
have ANYTHING YOU WISH TO HAVE,
be ANYTHING YOU WISH TO BE.

—ROBERT COLLIER

B U L L S E Y E ™

7" × 5"

paper dimensions

A   2½" × 4¾"
B   5¾" × 3½"
C   4" Circle (template 2)

instructions

1   Using a 7" × 5" card with the fold on the left side as your base, attach piece A to the card front placing it ½" from the bottom, keeping the left edges flush.

2   Attach piece B to the card front, placing it ½" from the top and left edges.

3   Attach piece C to the card front, placing it ¾" from the top, keeping the right edges flush.

4   Embellish as desired.

i d e a s ! *For more artwork featuring this pattern see page 99.*

C I T Y   S C A P E ™

4¾" × 3"

paper dimensions

A   4½" × ½"
B   3½" × 1¾"
C   2" × 1¼"
D   2¼" × 1½"

instructions

1   Using a 4¾" × 3" card with the fold on the left side as your base, attach piece A to the card front, placing it ⅛" from the top and left edge.

2   Attach piece B to the card front, placing it ½" from the bottom and ⅜" from the right edge.

3   Attach piece C to the center of piece D.

4   Attach piece D to the card front, placing it ¾" from the bottom and ⅛" from the right edge.

5   Embellish as desired.

i d e a s ! *For more artwork featuring this pattern see page 86.*

congratulations

congratulations

TIPS & TECHNIQUES
reverse rubber brayer

step 1 To reverse an image, roll rubber brayer over inked stamp.

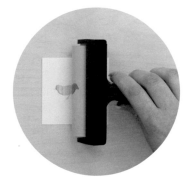

step 2 Roll brayer over cardstock.

paper dimensions

A 4" × 2½"
B 4" × 2½"
C 5" × 3"
D ½" × 6"
E 4" × 2"

instructions

1 Using a 6" × 6" card with the fold on the left side as your base, attach piece A to the card front, placing it ½" from the left side, keeping the top flush.

2 Attach piece B to the card front, placing it ½" from the right edge, keeping the bottom flush.

3 Attach piece C to the card front, placing it 1" from the left edge and ½" from the bottom.

4 Attach piece D to the card front, placing it ¾" from the bottom, keeping the side edges flush.

5 Attach piece E to the card front, placing it in the center of piece C.

6 Embellish as desired.

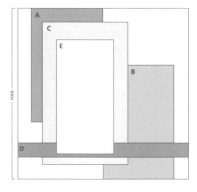

6" × 6"

ideas! *For more artwork featuring this pattern see page 96.*

For the pattern to Sentiment Secured (right) see page 78.

Jeanette's Tip

To create an aesthetically pleasing background pattern, randomly stamp images, evenly spaced, forming a repeating triangular pattern.

• • • D O W N   T H E   M I D D L E ™ • • •

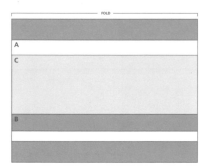

FOLD

A

C

B

4¼" × 5½"

ideas! *For more artwork featuring this pattern see pages 85 and 120.*

instructions

1 Using a 4¼" × 5½" card with the fold on the top as your base, attach piece A to the center of the card front, keeping the side edges flush.

2 Attach piece B to the card front, placing it 1" from the bottom, keeping the side edges flush.

3 Attach piece C to the card front, placing it 1" from the top, keeping the side edges flush.

4 Embellish as desired.

paper dimensions

A 3" × 5½"

B ¾" × 5½"

C 1¾" × 5½"

HE HAS ACHIEVED *success* WHO HAS LIVED WELL, LAUGHED OFTEN, AND *loved much.*

—BESSIE STANLEY

For the pattern to Box It Off
(right) see page 93.

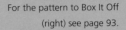

S I M P L E   S T R I P ™

instructions

1 Using a 3½" × 2½" card with the fold on the left as your base, attach piece A to the top of the card front, keeping the edges flush.

2 Attach piece B to the card front directly below piece A, keeping the edges flush.

3 Embellish as desired.

paper dimensions

A 1" × 2½"
B ½" × 2½"

3½" × 2½"

ideas! *For more artwork featuring this pattern see page 64.*

Jeanette's Tip

Use just a portion of a stamp's image by wiping ink off the areas of the image not needed prior to stamping.

My father DIDN'T TELL ME HOW TO LIVE; HE LIVED, AND LET ME *watch him* DO IT.

—CLARENCE BUDINTON KELLAND

TIPS & TECHNIQUES
dry embossing with stamps

step 1 Stamp image on the back of cardstock and go over with an embossing stylus.

step 2 Turn cardstock over and sand the embossed images with sandpaper.

paper dimensions

A	6" × 12"
B	5½" × 4"
C	3¾" × 3"
D	4" × 3¼"
E	3½" × ¾"
F	5½" × 1¾"

instructions

1 Using the Satchel template provided, score and fold piece A to form a 6" × 6" card base.

2 Attach piece B to the left flap of the card front, placing it ¼" from the top, keeping the side edges flush.

3 Attach piece C to the center of piece D.

4 Attach piece D to the center of the left flap of the card front, slightly angled.

5 Attach piece E to the center of piece F.

6 Attach piece F to the center of the right flap of the card front.

7 Embellish as desired.

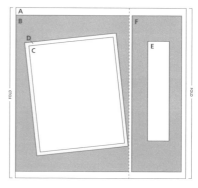

6" × 6"

ideas! *For more artwork featuring this pattern see page 82.*

father's day

CORNER SHOP ™

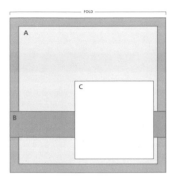

$4^{1}/_{2}$" × $4^{1}/_{2}$"

paper dimensions

A   4" × 4"
B $^{3}/_{4}$" × $4^{1}/_{2}$"
C $2^{1}/_{4}$" × $2^{1}/_{4}$"

ideas! *For more artwork featuring this pattern see pages 63 and 123.*

instructions

1   Using a $4^{1}/_{2}$" × $4^{1}/_{2}$" card with the fold on the top as your base, attach piece A to the center of the card front.

2   Attach piece B to the card front, placing it 1" from the bottom, keeping the side edges flush.

3   Attach piece C to the card front, placing it $^{1}/_{2}$" from the bottom and right edge.

4   Embellish as desired.

JUST RIGHT ™

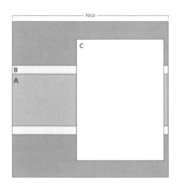

$4^{1}/_{2}$" × $4^{1}/_{2}$"

paper dimensions

A $1^{1}/_{2}$" × $4^{1}/_{2}$"
B   2" × $4^{1}/_{2}$"
C $3^{1}/_{2}$" × $2^{1}/_{2}$"

ideas! *For more artwork featuring this pattern see page 91.*

instructions

1   Attach piece A to the center of piece B, keeping the side edges flush.

2   Using a $4^{1}/_{2}$" × $4^{1}/_{2}$" card with the fold on the top as your base, attach piece B to the card front, placing it $1^{1}/_{4}$" from the top, keeping the side edges flush.

3   Attach piece C to the card front, placing it $^{1}/_{2}$" from the top and $^{1}/_{8}$" from the right edge.

4   Embellish as desired.

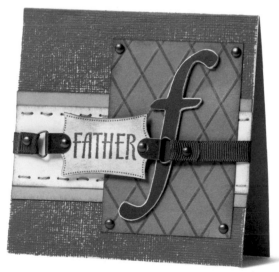

For the pattern to Middle Ground
(left) see page 19.

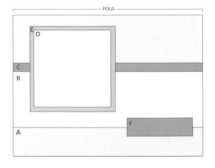

Jeanette's Tip

Create a multi-colored image by stamping the same image several times in different ink colors. Cut out pieces of each image and glue them to a stamped base image to form a combination of colors.

GOD GAVE ME THE *greatest gift* I EVER HAD,

GOD GAVE ME A BEST FRIEND IN THE FORM OF MY *dad.*

—ANONYMOUS

• • • SIMPLE EXPRESSION ™ • • •

paper dimensions

A   ¾" × 5½"
B   2" × 5½"
C   ¼" × 5½"
D   2¼" × 2¼"
E   2½" × 2½"
F   ¾" × 2"

instructions

1   Using a 4¼" × 5½" card with the fold on the top as your base, attach piece A to the bottom of the card front, keeping the edges flush.

2   Attach piece B to the card front directly above piece A, keeping the edges flush.

3   Attach piece C to the card front directly above piece B, keeping the edges flush.

4   Attach piece D to the center of piece E.

5   Attach piece E to the card front, placing it ⅜" from the top and left edge.

6   Attach piece F to the card front, placing it ¼" from the right edge and ⅜" from the bottom.

7   Embellish as desired.

4¼" × 5½"

ideas! *For more artwork featuring this pattern see page 95.*

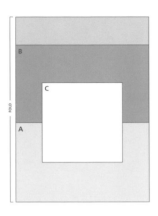

3¹/₂" × 2¹/₂"

paper dimensions

A 1¹/₂" × 2¹/₂"
B 1¹/₂" × 2¹/₂"
C 1¹/₂" × 1¹/₂"

instructions

1 Using a 3¹/₂" × 2¹/₂" card with the fold on the left side as your base, attach piece A to the bottom of the card front, keeping the edges flush.

2 Attach piece B to the card front, placing it directly above piece A, keeping the edges flush.

3 Attach piece C to the card front, placing it ¾" from the bottom and centered from side to side.

4 Embellish as desired.

ideas! *For more artwork featuring this pattern see page 78.*

A DAD IS SOMEONE TO LOOK *up to*

NO MATTER HOW TALL *you grow.*

TINY TABS ™

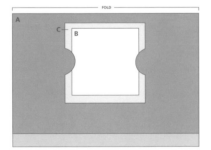

2¹/₂" × 3¹/₂"

paper dimensions

A 2¹/₄" × 3¹/₂"
B 1¹/₄" × 1¹/₄"
C 1¹/₂" × 1¹/₂"

ideas! *For more artwork featuring this pattern see page 102.*

instructions

1 Using the Tiny Tabs template provided, cut flaps in piece A.

2 Using a 2¹/₂" × 3¹/₂" card with the fold on the top as your base, attach piece A to the top of the card front, keeping the edges flush and making sure not to adhere the flaps.

3 Attach piece B to the center of piece C.

4 Attach piece C to the card front, tucking the side edges under the flaps in piece A.

5 Embellish as desired.

TIPS & TECHNIQUES
watercolor stamping

step 1 Ink the stamp. Spritz with a fine spray of water to achieve desired texture.

step 2 Press image to paper to reveal the watercolor look.

paper dimensions

A 5" × ¾"
B 3" × 1 ¾"
C 2½" × 2"

instructions

1 Using an 8" × 3½" card with the fold on the left side as your base, attach piece A to the card front, placing it ½" from the left edge, keeping the top flush.

2 Attach piece B to the card front, placing it ½" from the bottom and ¼" from the left edge.

3 Attach piece C to the card front, placing it ¼" from the bottom and right edge.

4 Embellish as desired.

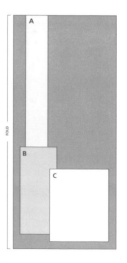

8" × 3½"

ideas! *For more artwork featuring this pattern see page 16.*

For the pattern to Collage
(left) see page 97.
For the pattern to File Pocket
(center) see page 89.
For the pattern to Layered Look
(right) see page 19.

Jeanette's Tip

Echo the good news from the front of your card by creating a mini envelope and announcement to accent the back of your card.

news

SPECIAL
A BOY!

SPECIAL
DELIVERY

Father-to-be

congratulations

daddy

baby

gratitude

Blessings

For the pattern to Keep it Level
see page 107.

For the pattern to
Enchanting Enclosure
(right) see page 31.

• • • T I M E L E S S   T R I O ™ • • •

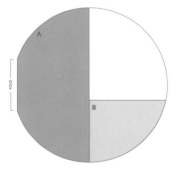

4½" circle

ideas! *For more artwork
featuring this pattern see page 102.*

instructions

1 Using the Timeless Trio templates
provided, trim pieces A and B.

2 Using a 4½" circle card (template 1)
with the fold on the left side as your base,
attach piece A to the left side of the card
front, keeping the edges flush.

3 Attach piece B to the bottom right side
of the card base, keeping the edges flush.

4 Embellish as desired.

paper dimensions

A 4½" × 2½"
B 2½" × 2½"

Jeanette's Tip

*Add that homemade
charm to your card with
hand-stitched accents.*

THERE IS A *calmness* TO A LIFE
LIVED IN GRATITUDE, A *quiet joy.*

—RALPH H. BLUM

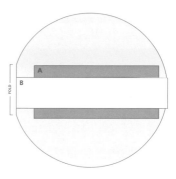

instructions

1 Using a 4½" circle card (template 1) with the fold on the left side as your base, attach piece A to the card front, placing it 1½" from the top and a ¼" from the right side.

2 Fold piece B, at 2¾" and 7¼", adhere the ends. Slide piece B over the card centered over piece A.

3 Embellish as desired.

4½" CIRCLE

paper dimensions

A   1½" × 3½"
B   ¾" × 10"

ideas! *For more artwork featuring this pattern see pages 65 and 123.*

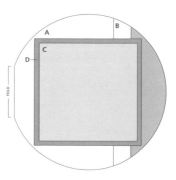

instructions

1 Using the Attention Getter template provided, trim piece A.

2 Using a 4½" circle card (template 1) with the fold on the left side as your base, attach piece A to the left side of the card front, keeping the edges flush.

3 Attach piece B to the card front, placing it directly to the right of piece A, keeping the edges flush. Trim the ends.

4 Attach piece C to the center of piece D.

5 Attach piece D to the center of the card front.

6 Embellish as desired.

4½" CIRCLE

paper dimensions

A   4½" × 3"
B   4½" × ½"
C   2¾" × 2¾"
D   3" × 3"

ideas! *For more artwork featuring this pattern see page 65.*

gratitude

step 1 Using a foam brush, apply paint liberally to stamp.

step 2 Stamp image on cardstock.

gratitude

instructions

1 Using the On the Ball templates provided, trim pieces A and B.

2 Using a 7" × 5" card with the fold on the left side as your base, attach piece A to the top left corner of the card front, keeping the straight edges flush.

3 Attach piece B to the bottom right corner of the card front, keeping the straight edges flush.

4 Attach piece C to the card front, placing it ¾" from the top and centered from side to side.

5 Embellish as desired.

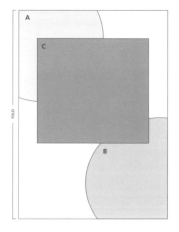

7" × 5"

ideas! *For more artwork featuring this pattern see page 95.*

paper dimensions

A   3¾" × 3"
B   3" × 3¾"
C   3 ¾" × 3½"

THREE TIERS ™

For the pattern to this card see page 66.

THREE WISHES ™

For the pattern to this card see page 109.

GEOMETRIC ™

For the pattern to this card see page 56.

GALLERY ™

For the pattern to this card see page 119.

For the pattern to All Squared Up (right) see page 101.

A CUT ABOVE™

FOLD

A

3" × 3"

ideas! *For more artwork featuring this pattern see page 93.*

instructions

1 Using a 3" × 3" card with the fold on the top as your base, attach piece A to the bottom of the card front, keeping the edges flush.

2 Embellish as desired.

paper dimensions

A 1¾" × 3"

Jeanette's Tip

Add flair to your clear embellishments by stamping on them with Staz-on™ ink. It is perfect for stamping on slick surfaces.

Gratitude IS THE *heart's memory.*

TIPS & TECHNIQUES
highlighting with the embossing pen

step 1   Color image with the embossing pen.

step 2   Coat with clear embossing powder and heat with craft heater.

paper dimensions

A	7½" × 3"
B	7¾" × 3¼"
C	2½" × 3"
D	½" × 3" (2)

instructions

1   Attach piece A to the center of piece B.

2   Using an 8" × 3½" card with the fold on the left side as your base, attach piece B to the center of the card front.

3   Attach piece C to the card front, placing it 1" from the top, keeping the side edges flush with piece A.

4   Attach one piece D slightly below the top of piece C, keeping the side edges flush. Attach the remaining piece D slightly above the bottom of piece C, keeping the side edges flush.

5   Embellish as desired.

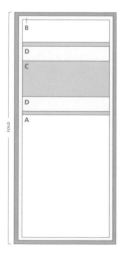

8" × 3½"

ideas! *For more artwork featuring this pattern see page 79.*

gratitude

For the pattern to Top View
(left) see page 86.
For the pattern to Keyhole
(right) see page 12.

Jeanette's Tip

*Step outside of the box by
stamping with lighter inks
on darker paper. Use paint or
lighter embossing powder for a
variation on this technique.*

TIPS & TECHNIQUES
stamping curved images
using the block buddy™

step 1 Place the Block Buddy™ on the block.

step 2 Arrange stamp along the line to match the contour of the image it should match.

gratitude

paper dimensions

A	4½" × 5"
B	1" × 5"
C	6" × 2½"
D	6¼" × 2¾"
E	2½" Circle (template 5)
F	3" Circle (template 4)

instructions

1 Using a 7" × 5" card with the fold on the left side as your base, attach piece A to the top of the card keeping the edges flush.

2 Attach piece B to the card front directly below piece A, keeping the edges flush.

3 Attach piece C to the center of piece D.

4 Attach piece D to the card front placing it ¼" from the right and centered from top to bottom.

5 Attach piece E to the center of piece F.

6 Attach piece F to the card front ⅝" from the bottom and ¼" from the left edge.

7 Embellish as desired.

7" × 5"

ideas! *For more artwork featuring this pattern see page 116.*

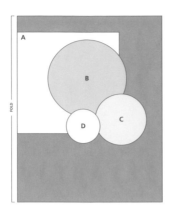

5½" × 4¼"

paper dimensions

A 3" × 3"
B 2½" Circle (template 5)
C 1½" Circle (template 7)
D 1" Circle (template 8)

instructions

1 Using a 5½" × 4¼" card with the fold on the left side as your base, attach piece A to the card front placing it ½" from the top keeping the left edge flush.

2 Attach pieces B, C, and D to the right side of piece A as desired to form a cluster.

3 Embellish as desired.

ideas! *For more artwork featuring this pattern see page 99.*

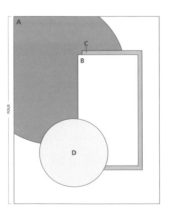

5½" × 4¼"

paper dimensions

A 4" × 3½"
B 3¼" × 1¾"
C 3½" × 1¾"
D 2" Circle (template 6)

instructions

1 Using the On the Edge template provided, trim piece A.

2 Using a 5½" × 4¼" card with the fold on the left side as your base, attach piece A to the top left corner of the card front, keeping the straight edges flush.

3 Attach piece B to piece C placing it ⅛" from the top and the right edges.

4 Attach piece C to the card front, placing it 1" from the top and ½" from the right edge.

5 Attach piece D to the card front, placing it ½" from the bottom and ¾" from the left edge.

6 Embellish as desired.

ideas! *For more artwork featuring this pattern see page 104.*

gratitude

For the pattern to Cubed Collage
see page 92.

For the pattern to Center Circles (left) see page 117.

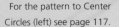

Jeanette's Tip

Make your images look like they are moving by inking once and stamping several times at a back angle.

S T A Y   L E F T ™

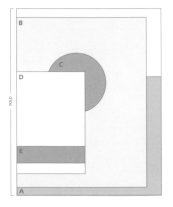

5½" × 4¼"

ideas! *For more artwork featuring this pattern see page 89.*

instructions

1 Using a 5½" × 4¼" card with the fold on the left side as your base, attach piece A to the bottom of the card front keeping the edges flush.

2 Attach piece B to the card front placing it ¼" from the top, keeping the left edges flush.

3 Attach piece C to piece B placing it 1" from the top and left edge.

4 Attach piece D to the card front placing it ½" from the bottom keeping the left edges flush.

5 Attach piece E to piece D, placing it ¼" from the bottom keeping the left edges flush.

6 Embellish as desired.

paper dimensions

A 3½" × 4¼"

B 5" × 4"

C 2" Circle (template 6)

D 3" × 2"

E ½" × 2"

HOPE YOUR *Halloween*

IS AS SWEET AS *you are!*

For the pattern to Windswept (left) see page 103.

October 31ˢᵗ, 2008

Join Us for a Spooky Event

Costume & Pumpkin Carving Contest

8 p.m. to midnight

Food and Fun

Happy Halloween

Bool

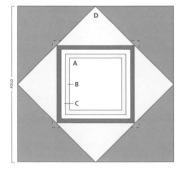

Jeanette's Tip

Create your own patterned ribbon by stamping on it! I stamped on black ribbon with white pigment ink.

• • • F O L D E D   F O C U S ™ • • •

paper dimensions

A $1\frac{1}{2}$ " × $1\frac{1}{2}$ "
B $1\frac{3}{4}$ " × $1\frac{3}{4}$ "
C   2" × 2"
D $4\frac{1}{2}$ " × $4\frac{1}{2}$ "

instructions

1   Using the Folded Focus template provided, trim and fold piece D.

2   Using a $4\frac{1}{2}$ " × $4\frac{1}{2}$ " card with the fold on the left side as your base, trim a $2\frac{1}{2}$ " × $2\frac{1}{2}$ " window from the center of the card front.

3   Attach piece A to the center of piece B.

4   Attach piece B to the center of piece C.

5   Attach piece C to the center of the card inside.

6   Attach piece D to the back of the card front, wrapping flaps through the window, and to the card front.

7   Embellish as desired.

$4\frac{1}{2}$ " × $4\frac{1}{2}$ "

ideas! *For more artwork featuring this pattern see page 91.*

Halloween IS HERE

WITH SPOOKY DISGUISES, PUMPKINS, AND BATS,

AND *scary surprises.*

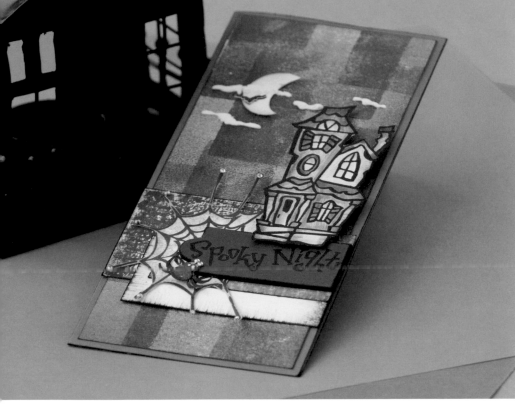

step 1 Ink a solid stamp or the back of a stamp, then stamp on an object with texture.

step 2 Stamp on cardstock to reveal the textured look.

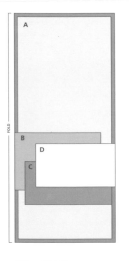

8" × 3½"

ideas! *For more artwork featuring this pattern see page 79.*

instructions

1 Using an 8" × 3½" card with the fold on the left as your base, attach piece A to the center of the card front.

2 Attach piece B to the card front, placing it 1½" from the bottom, keeping the left edges flush.

3 Attach piece C to the card front, placing it 1" from the bottom, keeping the right edges flush with piece A.

4 Attach piece D to the card front, placing it 1⅝" from the bottom, keeping the right edges flush.

5 Embellish as desired.

paper dimensions

A 7¾" × 3¼"
B 2" × 3"
C 1½" × 3"
D 1½" × 2¾"

For the pattern to Designer Tag
(top left) see page 97.
For the pattern to Mini Window
(bottom left) see page 105.
For the pattern to Done Right
(right) see page 119.

Jeanette's Tip

Accent the back of your card by creating a mini-landscape in one corner.

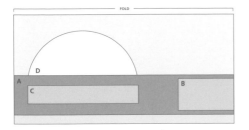

3" × 6"

paper dimensions

A   1" × 6"
B   1½" × ¾"
C   ½" × 3"
D   1½" × 3"

ideas! *For more artwork featuring this pattern see page 87.*

instructions

1   Using the Sunrise template provided, trim piece D.

2   Using a 3" × 6" card with the fold on the top as your base, attach piece A to the card front, placing it ¼" from the bottom, keeping the side edges flush.

3   Attach piece B centered top to bottom on piece A, keeping the right edges flush.

4   Attach piece C to the card front, placing it ½" from the bottom and left edge.

5   Attach piece D to the card front, placing it ½" from the left edge keeping the straight edge flush with the top of piece A.

6   Embellish as desired.

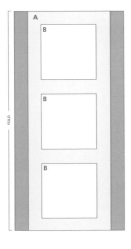

6" × 3"

paper dimensions

A   6" × 2¼"
B   1½" × 1½" (3)

instructions

1   Using a 6" × 3" card with the fold on the left side as your base, attach piece A to the center of the card front, keeping the top and bottom edges flush.

2   Attach pieces B to piece A, placing them ¼" from the top, ½" from each other, and centered from side to side.

3   Embellish as desired.

ideas! *For more artwork featuring this pattern see page 90.*

HAVE A *spooktacular* HALLOWEEN!

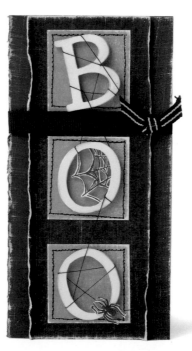

just because

For the pattern to Designer Tab
see page 125.

For the pattern to It's a Wrap (right) see page 12.

Jeanette's Tip

Use any stamped line image as a template for hand-stitched elements.

R O U N D A B O U T ™

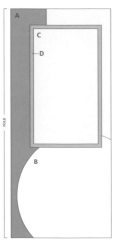

8" × 3½"

ideas! *For more artwork featuring this pattern see page 87.*

instructions

1 Using the Roundabout template provided, trim piece B.

2 Using an 8" × 3½" card with the fold on the left side as your base, attach piece A to the card front, keeping the left edge flush.

3 Attach piece B to the bottom right corner of the card front, keeping the straight edges flush.

4 Attach piece C to the center of piece D.

5 Attach piece D to the card front, placing it ½" from the top and ¼" from the right edge.

6 Embellish as desired.

paper dimensions

A 8" × 1¼"
B 4" × 3½"
C 4" × 2¼"
D 4¼" × 2½"

A joy SHARED IS A *joy doubled.*

— GOETHE

TIPS & TECHNIQUES
faux wax seal

just because

step 1 Coat paper with embossing ink and heat emboss ultra thick embossing powder onto paper, repeat 3–4 coats. Coat a stamp with a layer of embossing ink or paint; this will act as a release.

step 2 Heat an area of embossed layers as large as your stamp with the craft heater. While it's still hot, firmly press stamp into it.

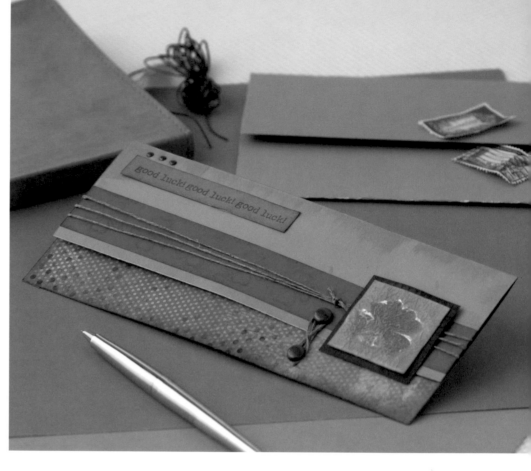

instructions

1 Fold piece A to create a 3½" × 8" card with the fold on the top.

2 Attach piece B to the card front, placing it 1⅜" from the top, keeping the side edges flush.

3 Attach piece C to the center of piece D.

4 Attach piece D to the card front, placing it 1" from the top and ½" from the right edge.

5 Attach piece E to the card front, placing it ¼" from the top and left edges.

6 Embellish as desired.

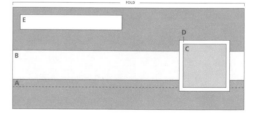

3½" × 8"

paper dimensions

A 6" × 8"
B 1" × 8"
C 1½" × 1½"
D 1¾" × 1¾"
E ½" × 3½"

ideas! *For more artwork featuring this pattern see page 87.*

For the pattern to Corner Shop (left) see page 39.
For the pattern to Ricochet (right) see page 127.

For the pattern to Simple Strip
(right) see page 37.

L E F T   E C L I P S E ™

instructions

paper dimensions

A   2" × 2"

1 Using the Left Eclipse template
provided, trim piece A.

2 Using a 3½ " × 2½ " card with the
fold on the left side as your base, attach
piece A to the bottom left corner of the
card front.

3 Embellish as desired.

i d e a s ! *For more artwork featuring this
pattern see pages 32 and 108.*

3½" × 2½"

One of the MOST BEAUTIFUL QUALITIES
OF TRUE FRIENDSHIP IS TO *understand*
AND *to be* UNDERSTOOD.

—LUCIUS ANNAEUS SENECA

S I D E   N O T E ™

For the pattern to this card see page 127.

S I M P L Y   S E C U R E ™

For the pattern to this card see page 46.

M E R R Y - G O - R O U N D ™

For the pattern to this card see page 30.

A T T E N T I O N   G E T T E R ™

For the pattern to this card see page 46.

For the pattern to
Mini Combination
(left) see page 84.

Jeanette's Tip

*Say what you want with style!
Combine multiple alphabet stamp
sets to create a sentiment that is
anywhere from sweet to funky—
and everything in-between.*

The world IS ROUND

SO THAT FRIENDSHIP MAY *encircle it.*

—PIERRE TEILHARD DE CHARDIN

• • • • **T H R E E   T I E R S** ™ • • • •

paper dimensions

A   1½" × 2½"
B   1" × 2"
C   ¾" × 1½"
D   ½" × ⅛"

instructions

1   Round the top two corners of pieces A, B, and C.

2   Using a 4¾" × 3" card with the fold on the left side as your base, attach piece A to the bottom of the card front, keeping the bottom flush and centered from side to side.

3   Attach piece B to the card front slightly overlapping the top of piece A and centered from side to side.

4   Attach piece C to the card front slightly overlapping the top of piece B and centered from side to side.

5   Attach piece D to the card front directly above piece C and centered from side to side.

6   Embellish as desired.

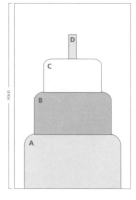

4 ¾" × 3"

ideas! *For more
artwork featuring this
pattern see pages 48 and 108.*

For the pattern to Simple
Statement (right) see page 11.

instructions

1 Using the Inner Court templates
provided, trim pieces B and C.

2 Using a 4½" circle card (template 1)
with the fold on the left side as your
base, attach piece A to the center of
the card front.

3 Attach piece B to the right side of
piece A, keeping the edges flush.

4 Attach piece C directly to the left of
piece B, keeping the edges flush.

5 Attach piece D to the card front,
placing it 1" from the top and ½" from
the right edge.

6 Embellish as desired.

paper dimensions

A 4" Circle (template 2)
B 4" × 1¼"
C 4" × ½"
D 2½" Circle (template 5)

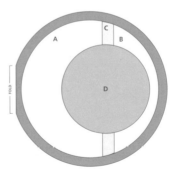

4½" circle

ideas! *For more artwork featuring*
this pattern see pages 30 and 123.

You don't need a reason to get or give a card—sometimes the best reason of all is "just because!" In this fun card workshop, you can create 20 dramatic cards (two each of ten designs) in the standard 5½" × 4¼" size, using just six sheets of paper plus card bases. Here's what you'll need to get started:

12" × 12" cardstock (4)
12" × 12" Background and Texture papers (2)
5½" × 4¼" card bases (20)

For this card workshop, you can use pre-cut standard card bases, or easily make your own. To make your own card bases, you'll need 10 sheets of 8½" × 11" cardstock in colors that coordinate with your accent cardstocks and Background and Texture papers. Cut each sheet of 8½" × 11" cardstock in half (width-wise), score at the center of each cut piece and fold. Voilà! A perfect card base in seconds. Next, follow the cutting diagrams and assembly instructions and embellish to your heart's delight. For these samples, a sparkle of rhinestones and the ridges of ricrac, together with a sprinkle of stamped sentiments and images, bring the look together. And here's a helpful tip: use your cardstock scraps left from the cutting diagrams for stamping great images you can paper-piece onto the cards. Quick, easy, and economical! Finish it off with envelopes made easy—a coordinating envelope template is on the included CD . . . just because!

CARDSTOCK

CARDSTOCK *

CARDSTOCK *

CARDSTOCK

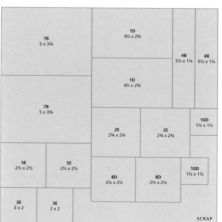

B & T PAPER

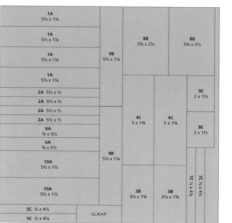

B & T PAPER

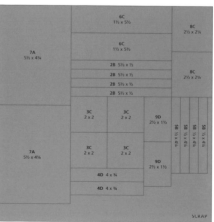

*Identical papers

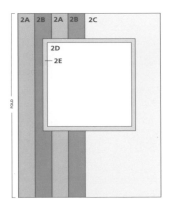

5½" × 4¼"

paper dimensions

1A 5½" × 1⅛" (2)
1B 5½" × 2"
1C 4¼" × 2½"
1D 4½" × 2¾"

instructions

1 Using a 5½" × 4¼" card with the fold on the left side as your base, attach one piece 1A to the left side of the card front, keeping the edges flush. Attach remaining piece 1A to the right side of the card front, keeping the edges flush.

2 Attach piece 1B to the center of the card front.

3 Attach piece 1C to the center of piece 1D.

4 Attach piece 1D to the center of the card front.

5 Embellish as desired.

5½" × 4¼"

paper dimensions

2A 5½" × ½" (2)
2B 5½" × ½" (2)
2C 5½" × 2¼"
2D 2½" × 2½"
2E 2¾" × 2¾"

instructions

1 Using a 5½" × 4¼" card with the fold on the left side as your base, attach pieces 2A and 2B, alternating from the left side of the card, keeping the edges flush.

2 Attach piece 2C to the right side of the card front, keeping the edges flush.

3 Attach piece 2D to the center of piece 2E.

4 Attach piece 2E to the card front, placing it ¾" from the top and right edges.

5 Embellish as desired.

C A R D 3

instructions

1 Using a 5½" × 4¼" card with the fold on the left side as your base, attach piece 3A to the card front.

2 Attach piece 3B to the card front, placing it ½" from the top and left edges.

3 Attach one piece 3C to the card front, placing it ¾" from the top and left edges. Attach remaining piece 3C to the card front, placing it 1¼" from the top and 1½" from the left edge.

4 Attach piece 3D to the center of piece 3E.

5 Attach piece 3E to the card front, placing it 1" from the top and 1¼" from the left edge.

6 Embellish as desired.

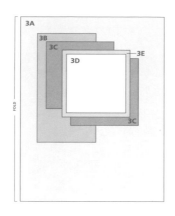

5½" × 4¼"

paper dimensions

3A 5½" × 4¼"
3B 3¼" × 1¾"
3C 2" × 2" (2)
3D 1¾" × 1¾"
3E 2" × 2"

C A R D 4

instructions

1 Using a 5½" × 4¼" card with the fold on the left side as your base, attach piece 4A to the card front.

2 Attach piece 4B to the card front, placing it 1¼" from the right edge, keeping the top and bottom flush.

3 Attach piece 4C to the card front, placing it ¼" from the right edge, keeping the top flush.

4 Attach piece 4D to the card front, placing it 1½" from the right edge, keeping the top flush.

5 Attach piece 4E to the card front, placing it ½" from the top and ¾" from the right edge.

6 Embellish as desired.

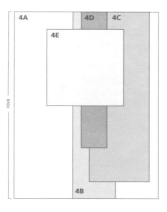

5½" × 4¼"

paper dimensions

4A 5½" × 4¼"
4B 5½" × 1¼"
4C 5" × 1¾"
4D 4" × ¾"
4E 2¼" × 2¼"

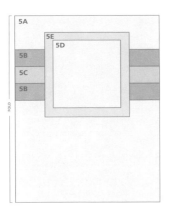

5½" × 4¼"

paper dimensions

5A   5½" × 4¼"
5B   ½" × 4¼" (2)
5C   ½" × 4¼"
5D   2" × 2"
5E   2½" × 2½"

instructions

1   Using a 5½" × 4¼" card with the fold on the left side as your base, attach piece 5A to the card front.

2   Attach pieces 5B and 5C, alternating, to the card front, placing them 1" from the top, keeping the side edges flush.

3   Attach piece 5D to the center of piece 5E.

4   Attach piece 5E to the card front, placing it ½" from the top and centered side to side.

5   Embellish as desired.

4¼" × 5½"

paper dimensions

6A   ¾" × 5½"
6B   2" × 5½"
6C   1½" × 5½"

instructions

1   Using a 4¼" × 5½" card with the fold on the top as your base, attach piece 6A to the top of the card front, keeping the edges flush.

2   Attach piece 6B to the card front, directly below piece 6A, keeping the edges flush.

3   Attach piece 6C to the bottom of the card front, keeping the edges flush.

4   Embellish as desired.

C A R D 7

instructions

1 Using a 5½" × 4¼" card with the fold on the left side as your base, attach piece 7A to the card front.

2 Attach piece 7B to the center of the card front.

3 Attach piece 7C to the card front, placing it 1¼" from the bottom, keeping the side edges flush.

4 Attach piece 7D to the card front, placing it 1" from the bottom and centered side to side.

5 Embellish as desired.

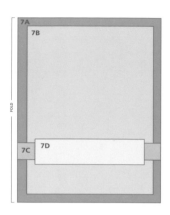

$5^{1}/_{2}$" × $4^{1}/_{4}$"

paper dimensions

7A 5½" × 4¼"
7B 5" × 3 ¾"
7C ½" × 4¼"
7D ¾" × 3¼"

C A R D 8

instructions

1 Using a 5½" × 4¼" card with the fold on the left side as your base, attach piece 8A to the card front.

2 Attach piece 8B to the card front, placing it ¼" from the bottom and right edges.

3 Attach piece 8C to the card front, placing it ¼" from the top and left edges.

4 Using Circle 4 template provided, trim piece 8D. Attach to the card front, placing it 1¾" from the top and ¾" from the left edge.

5 Embellish as desired.

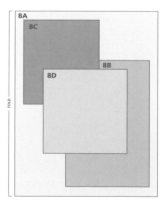

$5^{1}/_{2}$" × $4^{1}/_{4}$"

paper dimensions

8A 5½" × 4¼"
8B 3¾" × 2½"
8C 2½" × 2¼"
8D 2½" × 2½"

9A 9B 9C
9D
9E
9F

FOLD

5½" × 4¼"

paper dimensions

9A 5½" × 1½"
9B 5½" × 1¼"
9C 5½" × 1½"
9D 2½" × 1½"
9E 2" × 1½"
9F 2¼" × 1½"

instructions

1 Using a 5½" × 4¼" card with the fold on the left side as your base, attach piece 9A to the left side of the card front, keeping the edges flush.

2 Attach piece 9B to the card front, placing it directly beside piece 9A, keeping the edges flush.

3 Attach piece 9C to the right side of the card front, keeping the edges flush.

4 Attach piece 9D to the card front, placing it ¾" from the top and ½" from the left edge.

5 Attach piece 9E to the card front, placing it 1" from the top and right edges.

6 Attach piece 9F to the card front, placing it 1¼" from the top and 1⅜" from the right edge.

7 Embellish as desired.

10B 10A
10D
10C

FOLD

10E

5½" × 4¼"

paper dimensions

10A 5½" × 1½"
10B 5½" × 3"
10C 1¼" × 1¼"
10D 1½" × 1½"
10E 1" × 3"

instructions

1 Using a 5½" × 4¼" card with the fold on the left side as your base, trim 1¼" from the right side of the card front.

2 Attach piece 10A to the right, inside of the card, keeping the edges flush.

3 Attach piece 10B to the card front.

4 Attach piece 10C to the center of piece 10D.

5 Attach piece 10D to the card front, placing it ¾" from the top and left edges.

6 Cut two 1¼" slits ¼" apart in the card front ⅜" from the bottom and ½" from the right edge.

7 Attach ½" of piece 10E to the card back, placing it ½" from the bottom. Fold over to the card front and slide through the slits.

8 Embellish as desired.

mother's day

HAPPY MOTHER'S DAY

For the pattern to Confidential
see page 122.

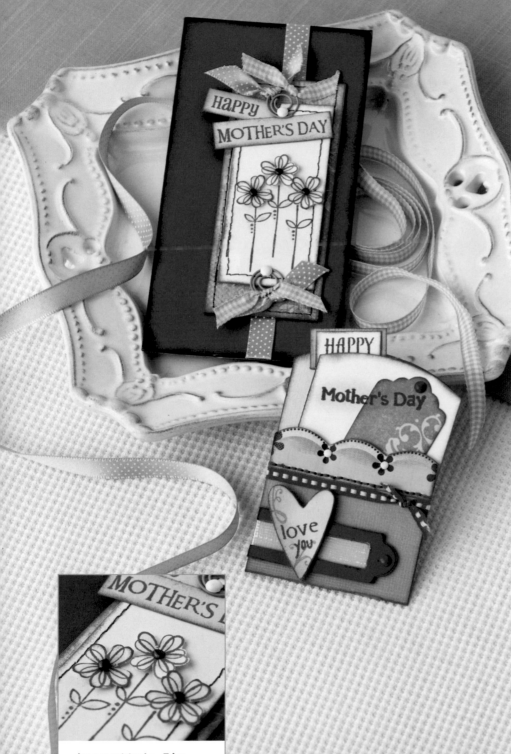

instructions

1 Using the Keep It Secret template A provided, trim and fold piece A, adhering the side tabs in order to create a pocket card.

2 Using the Keep It Secret template B provided, trim piece B.

3 Attach one end of Ribbon C to the back of piece B, centering it from side to side. Fold over the card front and attach, creating a loop.

4 Insert piece B into piece A pocket.

5 Embellish as desired.

paper dimensions

A   3½" × 5¾"
B   2½" × 3¼"
C   Ribbon 1½"

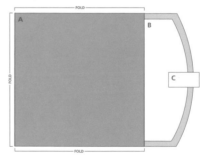

2½" × 3½"

ideas! *For more artwork featuring this pattern see page 105.*

Jeanette's Tip

Add subtle hues to an image by coloring it in with chalk using a sponge applicator.

For the pattern to Name Plate (top) see page 18.

A mother's BUSINESS IS *love.*

instructions

1 Using the Fancy Four template provided, trim piece D.

2 Using a 4½" × 4½" card with the fold on the left side as your base, attach piece A to the card front placing it ¼" from the top and right edge.

3 Attach piece B to the card front placing it ½" from the top and right edge.

4 Attach piece C to the card front placing it ½" from the bottom and ¾" from the right edge.

5 Attach piece D to the top of piece B slightly angled.

6 Embellish as desired.

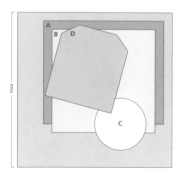

4½" × 4½"

paper dimensions

A 3" × 3½"
B 3" × 3"
C 1½" Circle (template 7)
D 2¼" × 2"

ideas! *For more artwork featuring this pattern see page 13.*

For my MOTHER and my FRIEND

instructions

1 Using the Matchbook template provided, trim and fold piece A to form the card base.

2 Attach piece B to the center of piece C.

3 Attach piece C to the card front, placing it ¼" from the top and left edge.

4 Embellish as desired.

ideas! *For more artwork featuring this pattern see pages 28 and 123.*

4½" × 4½"

paper dimensions

A 4½" × 9¾"
B 3¾" × 3"
C 4" × 3¼"

TIPS & TECHNIQUES
popping a stamped image

step 1 Using a cutting mat and a cutting knife, cut along details of a stamped image, making sure to leave connecting points for stability.

step 2 Gently lift and bend the cut areas to add dimension.

instructions

1 Attach piece A to the center of piece B.

2 Attach piece B to the center of piece C.

3 Using a 7" × 5" card with the fold on the left as your base, attach piece C to the center of the card front.

4 Embellish as desired.

paper dimensions

A   5" × 3"
B   5½" × 3½"
C   6¼" × 4¼"

7" × 5"

ideas! *For more artwork featuring this pattern see page 36.*

Motherhood:
ALL LOVE *begins and ends* THERE.

—ROBERT BROWNING

For the pattern to Three In a Row
(right) see page 41.

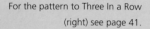

Jeanette's Tip

Freshen up your cards by stamping on fun textures such as linen.

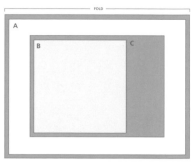

• • • S E N T I M E N T   S E C U R E D ™ • • •

instructions

1 Using a 4¼" × 5½" card with the fold on the top as your base, attach piece A to the center of the card front.

2 Attach piece B to piece C, placing it ⅛" from the top and left edges.

3 Attach piece C to the card front, placing it ⅝" from the top and right edges.

4 Embellish as desired.

paper dimensions

A 4 " × 5¼"
B 2¾" × 2¾"
C 3" × 4"

4¼" × 5½"

ideas! *For more artwork featuring this pattern see page 35.*

God's MOST PRECIOUS WORK OF ART
IS THE *warmth* AND LOVE
OF A *mother's heart.*

SIMPLY SAID™

For the pattern to this card see page 17.

TOP IT OFF™

For the pattern to this card see page 30.

TOP BAND™

For the pattern to this card see page 100.

LOWER LAYERS™

For the pattern to this card see page 57.

TIPS & TECHNIQUES
over stamping

step 1 Stamp one image on your cardstock in a light color.

step 2 Stamp a second image in a darker color directly over the first image.

paper dimensions

A 3" × 5"
B 12" Ribbon
C 3¼" × 3¼"
D 3½" × 3½"

instructions

1 Trim the corners off the right side of piece A to create a tag.

2 Wrap ribbon B around piece A. Tie a knot on the right side and trim ends.

3 Using a 6" × 6" card with the fold on the left side as your base, attach piece A to the card front, placing it ½" from the bottom, keeping the left edges flush.

4 Attach piece C to the center of piece D.

5 Attach piece D to the card front, placing it ¾" from the bottom and ¼" from the left edge.

6 Embellish as desired.

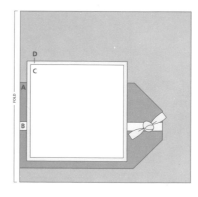

6" × 6"

ideas! *For more artwork featuring this pattern see page 13.*

mother's day

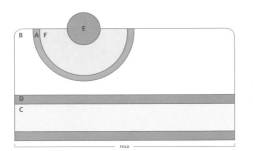

3" × 6"

paper dimensions

A   6" × 6"
B   3" × 6"
C   ¾" × 6"
D   1¼" × 6"
E   1" Circle (template 8)
F   2¾" × 5"

ideas! *For more artwork featuring this pattern see pages 18 and 126.*

instructions

1   Using the Fancy File template A provided, trim and fold piece A to form the 6" × 3" card base with the fold on the bottom.

2   Using the Fancy File template B provided, trim piece B. Attach piece B to the card front, keeping the edges flush.

3   Attach piece C to the center of piece D, keeping the side edges flush.

4   Attach piece D to the bottom of the card front, keeping the edges flush.

5   Attach piece E to the top of piece F, placing it 1" from the left edge, leaving half of the circle off of the edge creating a tab.

6   Place insert F inside card.

7   Embellish as desired.

MY *mother,* MY *friend.*

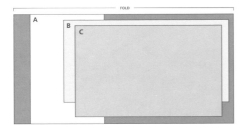

3" × 6"

paper dimensions

A   2" × 3"
B   4½" × 2¼"
C   4" × 2½"

ideas! *For more artwork featuring this pattern see page 90.*

instructions

1   Using a 6" × 3" card with the fold on the top as your base, attach piece A to the card front, placing it ½" from the left edge keeping the top and bottom flush.

2   Attach piece B to the card front, placing it ⅛" from the top and ¼" from the right edge.

3   Attach piece C to the card front, placing it ⅜" from the top and ½" from the right edge.

4   Embellish as desired.

new year's

3! 2! 1!

Happy New Year!

For the pattern to Satchel see page 38.

step 1 Stamp the solid or base image.

step 2 Stamp the outline or shade image over the top of the base image.

instructions

1 Using an 8″ × 3½″ card with the fold on the left as your base, cut a 2½″ × 2½″ square in the card front ¼″ from the top and right edge.

2 Attach piece A to the inside card back, placing it ¼″ from the top and right edge.

3 Embellish as desired.

paper dimensions

A 2½″ × 2½″

8″ × 3½″

ideas! *For more artwork featuring this pattern see page 90.*

A new year OF MEMORIES
IS IN THE *making.*

new year's

instructions

1 Using a 3" × 3" card with the fold on the top as your base, attach piece A to the top of the card front, keeping the edges flush.

2 Attach piece B to the card front, placing it ¼" from the top, keeping the right edges flush.

3 Attach piece C to the card front, placing it ⅜" from the top, keeping the right edges flush.

4 Attach piece D to the center of piece E.

5 Attach piece E to the card front, placing it ½" from the top and ¼" from the right edge.

6 Embellish as desired.

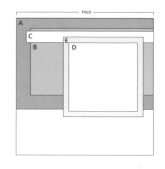

3" × 3"

paper dimensions

A 2" × 3"
B 1½" × 2¾"
C ¼" × 2⅞"
D 1½" × 1½"
E 1¾" × 1¾"

ideas! *For more with this pattern see page 66.*

instructions

1 Using a 3" × 3" card with the fold on the left side as your base, attach piece A to the card front, placing it ½" from the right edge, keeping the top and bottom flush.

2 Attach piece B to the card front, placing it ½" from the top and ¼" from the right edge.

3 Embellish as desired.

ideas! *For more artwork featuring this pattern see page 28.*

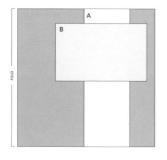

3" × 3"

paper dimensions

A 3" × 1"
B 1¼" × 2"

new year's

For the pattern to Circle Collection
(left) see page 29.

For the pattern to Down the Middle
(right) see page 35.

For the pattern to Circle Collection
(left) see page 29.

For the pattern to Down the Middle
(right) see page 35.

Jeanette's Tip

*Create a delicate feel for the inside
of your card by stamping overlapping images in light inks. Write
your sentiment directly over your
stamping.*

For the pattern to City Scape (right) see page 33.

For the pattern to City Scape (right) see page 33.

T O P   V I E W ™

CHEERS TO A *new year* OF HOPE AND *possibilities!*

paper dimensions

A   2½" × 2½"
B   9" Ribbon

instructions

1   Using 3" × 8½" card with the fold on the top as your base, attach piece A to the card front, placing it ⅝" from the left and centered from top to bottom.

2   Tie ribbon B around the card front. Tie in a knot and trim ends.

3   Embellish as desired.

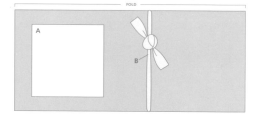

3½" × 8"

ideas! *For more artwork featuring this pattern see page 51.*

For more artwork featuring this pattern see page 51.

For the pattern to Roundabout
(bottom left) see page 61.
For the pattern to Sunrise
(top left) see page 59.
For the pattern to Classic Closure
(right) see page 62.

Jeanette's Tip

*Decorate the back of your card like
I did here with a sentiment that is
appropriate to the card theme.*

Here's
to the
Future!

HAPPY
NEW
YEAR!

new
year

2010

patriotic

For the pattern to Simplicity
see page 106.

For the pattern to Stay Left
(left) see page 55.

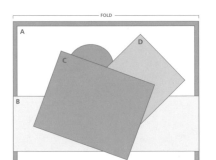

4¼" × 5½"

ideas! *For more artwork
featuring this pattern see page 43.*

FILE POCKET ™

instructions

1 Using the File Pocket template provided, trim and fold piece C to create a folder.

2 Using a 4¼" × 5½" card with the fold on the top as your base, attach piece A to the center of the card front.

3 Attach piece B to the card front, placing it ½" from the bottom, keeping the side edges flush.

4 Attach the back of piece C to the card front, slightly angled.

5 Attach piece D to the card front, slightly angled and inside the flap of piece C.

6 Embellish as desired.

paper dimensions

A   4" × 5¼"

B   1½" × 5½"

C   3" × 5"

D   2" × 3"

WHERE *liberty* DWELLS,
THERE IS *my country.*

—BENJAMIN FRANKLIN

FREEDOM

July

GOD ★ BLESS ★ AMERICA

For the pattern to Long Layers
(left) see page 81.
For the pattern to Simple Side View
(top right) see page 83.
For the pattern to All Stacked Up
(bottom right) see page 59.

UP IN THE CORNER™

For the pattern to this card see page 121.

FOLDED FOCUS™

For the pattern to this card see page 56.

WINDOW WISHES™

For the pattern to this card see page 121.

JUST RIGHT™

For the pattern to this card see page 39.

patriotic

natriotic

TIPS & TECHNIQUES
ghosting

step 1 Emboss design on a light piece of cardstock. With a darker color, ink over the design.

step 2 Lay a scrap piece of cardstock over the top of the embossed design and iron. The heat of the iron will transfer the embossing powder from your design to the scrap piece of paper, leaving a ghosted image.

instructions

1 Using a 7" × 5" card with the fold on the left side as your base, attach piece A to the card front, placing it 1" from the top and ¼" from the right edge.

2 Attach piece B to the card front, placing it ½" from the top and left edge.

3 Attach piece C to the card front, placing it ¾" from the top and right edge.

4 Embellish as desired.

paper dimensions

A 3½" × 3½"
B 3½" × 3½"
C 3" × 3"

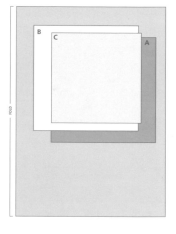

7" × 5"

ideas! *For more artwork featuring this pattern see page 54.*

For the pattern to A Cut Above
(right) see page 49.

B O X   I T   O F F ™

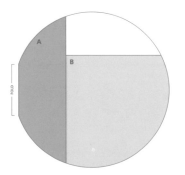

4½" circle

ideas! *For more artwork featuring this pattern see page 37.*

instructions

1 Using the Box it Off templates provided, trim pieces A and B.

2 Using a 4½" circle card (template 1) with the fold on the left side as your base, attach piece A to the left side of the card front, keeping the edges flush.

3 Attach piece B to the bottom right of the card front, keeping the edges flush.

4 Embellish as desired.

paper dimensions

A 4¼" × 1½"
B 3½" × 3¼"

Jeanette's Tip

Accent your card with a unique technique by stamping directly on clay.

THIS IS *my country,*

LAND THAT *I love.*

instructions

1 Using a 4½" × 4½" card with the fold on the top as your base, attach piece A to the card front, placing it ½" from the right edge, keeping the top and bottom flush.

2 Attach piece B to the card front, placing it ¾" from the right edge, keeping the top and bottom flush.

3 Attach piece C to the center of piece D.

4 Attach piece D to the card front, placing it ¼" from the top and ⅝" from the right edge.

5 Embellish as desired.

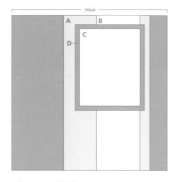

4½" × 4½"

paper dimensions

A	4½" × 2½"
B	4½" × 1¼"
C	2¼" × 1¾"
D	2½" × 2"

ideas! *For more artwork featuring this pattern see page 13.*

instructions

1 Using a 4½" × 4½" card with the fold on the top as your base, attach piece A to the center of the card front.

2 Fold piece B, at 2" and 6 ⅝", adhere the ends. Slide piece B over the card ½" from the bottom.

3 Attach piece C to piece B, placing it ⅜" from the right edge and ⅛" from the bottom.

4 Embellish as desired.

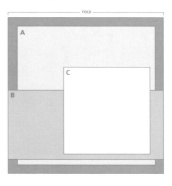

4½" × 4½"

paper dimensions

A	4" × 4"
B	2" × 10"
C	2½" × 2½"

ideas! *For more artwork featuring this pattern see page 104.*

patriotic

For the pattern to Simple Expression
(left) see page 40.
For the pattern to On the Ball
(right) see page 47.

Jeanette's Tip

*Quickly add colored detail to a
lightly stamped image by high-
lighting portions with a marker.*

season's greetings

For the pattern to
Pieced Together see page 34.

DESIGNER TAG™

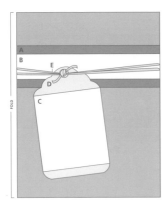

$5^{1}/_{2}" \times 4^{1}/_{4}"$

paper dimensions

A $1^{1}/_{4}" \times 4^{1}/_{4}"$
B $^{3}/_{4}" \times 4^{1}/_{4}"$
C $2^{1}/_{4}" \times 2"$
D $3^{1}/_{4}" \times 2"$
E   27" Fiber

instructions

1   Using the Designer Tag template provided, trim piece D and punch a hole in the top.

2   Using a $5^{1}/_{2}" \times 4^{1}/_{4}"$ card with the fold on the left side as your base, attach piece A to the card front 1" from the top, keeping side edges flush.

3   Attach piece B to the center of piece A, keeping the side edges flush.

4   Attach piece C to piece D, $^{1}/_{4}"$ from the bottom, keeping the side edges flush.

5   Fold fiber E in half, wrap around the card front, and thread through the hole in piece D. Tie a knot and trim ends.

6   Embellish as desired.

ideas! *For more artwork featuring this pattern see page 58.*

COLLAGE™

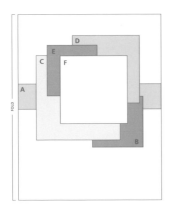

$5^{1}/_{2}" \times 4^{1}/_{4}"$

paper dimensions

A $^{3}/_{4}" \times 4^{1}/_{4}"$
B $1^{1}/_{2}" \times 1^{1}/_{2}"$
C $2^{1}/_{2}" \times 2^{1}/_{2}"$
D $2" \times 2"$
E $1^{1}/_{2}" \times 1^{1}/_{2}"$
F $2" \times 2"$

instructions

1   Using a $5^{1}/_{2}" \times 4^{1}/_{4}"$ card with the fold on the left side as your base, attach piece A to the card front, placing it $2^{1}/_{4}"$ from the top, keeping the side edges flush.

2   Attach piece B to the card front, placing it $^{1}/_{2}"$ from the right edge and $1^{1}/_{4}"$ from the bottom.

3   Attach piece C to the card front, placing it $1^{1}/_{2}"$ from the top and $^{1}/_{2}"$ from the left side.

4   Attach piece D to the card front, placing it 1" from the top and $^{5}/_{8}"$ from the right edge.

5   Attach piece E to the card front, placing it $1^{1}/_{4}"$ from the top and $^{3}/_{4}"$ from the left edge.

6   Attach piece F to the card front, placing it $1^{1}/_{2}"$ from the top and 1" centered from side to side.

7   Embellish as desired.

ideas! *For more artwork featuring this pattern see page 43.*

season's greetings

season's greetings

TIPS & TECHNIQUES
stamping on vellum

step 1 Randomly stamp vellum.

step 2 Use a heat tool at a distance, keeping the heat moving to completely dry the ink.

paper dimensions
A 6" × 6"
B 6" × 6"

instructions

1 Using a 6" × 6" card with the fold on the left side as your base attach piece A to the inside back of the card.

2 Cut a 4" circle (template 2) from the center of piece B. Attach piece B to the card front, keeping the edges flush.

3 Cut a 3½" circle (template 3) from the center of the card front.

4 Embellish as desired.

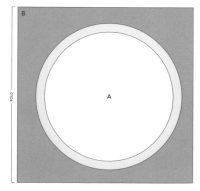

6" × 6"

ideas! *For more artwork featuring this pattern see page 26.*

Jeanette's Tip

Give your images even more definition by applying chalk to images stamped with a watermark stamp pad.

For the pattern to
Delightful Dots (top) see page 53.
For the pattern to
Bullseye (bottom) see page 33.

TIPS & TECHNIQUES
aging textured cardstock

step 1 Load a stipple brush with re-inker, dabbing off excess ink until desired amount is remaining. Brush on ink toward the edges of the paper.

step 2 Using an almost dry stipple brush, daub the outside edges of the cardstock.

season's greetings

paper dimensions

A 8" × 3"
B 4½" × 2½"
C 1" × 3½"

instructions

1 Using an 8" × 3½" card with the fold on the left as your base, attach piece A to the left side of the card front, keeping the edges flush.

2 Attach piece B to the card front, placing it 1" from the top, keeping the left edges flush.

3 Attach piece C to the card front, placing it 1¾" from the top, keeping the side edges flush.

4 Embellish as desired.

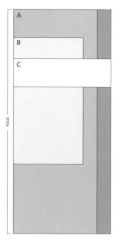

8" × 3½"

ideas! *For more artwork featuring this pattern see page 79.*

ALL SQUARED UP ™

4¹⁄₂" × 4¹⁄₂"

paper dimensions

A 4¹⁄₄ × 4¹⁄₄"
B 2¹⁄₂" × 2¹⁄₂"
C 2³⁄₄" × 2³⁄₄"

instructions

1 Using a 4¹⁄₂" × 4¹⁄₂" card with the fold on the top as your base, attach piece A to the center of the card front.

2 Attach piece B to the center of piece C.

3 Attach piece C to the center of the card front.

4 Embellish as desired.

ideas! *For more artwork featuring this pattern see page 19.*

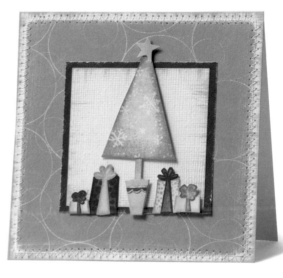

SMALL WONDER ™

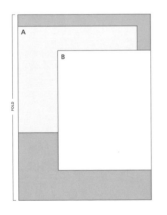

3¹⁄₂" × 2¹⁄₂"

paper dimensions

A 2" × 2¹⁄₄"
B 2¹⁄₄" × 1³⁄₄"

instructions

1 Using a 3¹⁄₂" × 2¹⁄₂" card with the fold on the left side as your base, attach piece A to the card front, placing it ¹⁄₄" from the top, keeping the left edges flush.

2 Attach piece B to the card front, placing it ³⁄₄" from the top, keeping the right edges flush.

3 Embellish as desired.

ideas! *For more artwork featuring this pattern see page 124.*

season's greetings

Joy

to the world

O Come Let Us Adore Him

Blessed IS THE SEASON

WHICH *engages* THE WHOLE WORLD

IN A CONSPIRACY OF *love.*

— HAMILTON WRIGHT MABIE

For the pattern to Tiny Tabs
(left) see page 41.
For the pattern to Timeless Trio
(right) see page 45.

step 1 Ink your stamp with desired color and stamp directly on twill.

step 2 To add texture, rub ink into the twill and highlight using colored pencils.

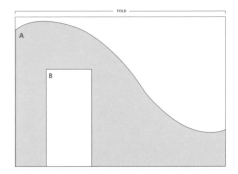

5" × 7"

i d e a s ! *For more artwork featuring this pattern see page 56.*

instructions

1 Using the Windswept template provided, trim piece A.

2 Using a 5" × 7" card with the fold on the top as your base, attach piece A to the bottom of the card front, keeping the straight edges flush.

3 Attach piece B to the card front, placing it 1" from the left side, keeping the bottom flush.

4 Embellish as desired.

paper dimensions

A 5" × 7"
B 3¼" × 1½"

For the pattern to On the Edge
(top) see page 53.
For the pattern to All Tucked In
(bottom) see page 94.

For the pattern to Keep It Secret (right) see page 75.

M I N I   W I N D O W ™

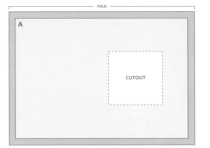

2½" × 3½"

i d e a s ! *For more artwork featuring this pattern see page 58.*

instructions

1 Using a 2½" × 3½" card with the fold on the top as your base, attach piece A to the center of the card front.

2 Cut a 1" × 1" square from the card front, ¾" from the top and ½" from the right side.

3 Embellish as desired.

paper dimensions

A 2¼" × 3¼"

Wishing you A HOLIDAY SEASON
FILLED *with love.*

For the pattern to Sun Dial
(right) see page 14.

Jeanette's Tip

*Stamping metal accents with a
non-porous ink is the perfect way
to add a professional touch to
your card.*

ENJOY *the sights
and sounds* OF THE SEASON.

S I M P L I C I T Y ™

paper dimensions

A 1½" × 5"
B 2" × 2"

instructions

1 Using a 7" × 5" card with the fold on
the left side as your base, attach piece A
to the card front, placing it 1¾" from the
top, keeping the side edges flush.

2 Attach piece B to the card front,
placing it ½" from the left edge and
1½" from the top.

3 Embellish as desired.

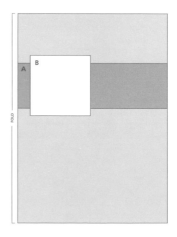

7" × 5"

ideas! *For more artwork
featuring this pattern see page 88.*

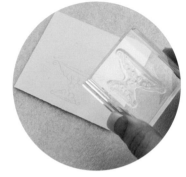

step 1 Stamp image in a light color and trace with colored pencil.

step 2 Shade image by using varying pressure on colored pencils to achieve different color intensity.

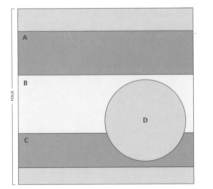

6" × 6"

ideas! *For more artwork featuring this pattern see page 44.*

instructions

1 Using a 6" × 6" card with the fold on the left side as the base, attach piece A to the card front placing it ¾" from the top keeping the side edges flush.

2 Attach piece B to the card front directly below piece A keeping the edges flush.

3 Attach piece C to the card front directly below piece B keeping the edges flush.

4 Attach piece D to the card front placing it ¼" from the right edge and ⅝" from the bottom.

5 Embellish as desired.

paper dimensions

A 1½" × 6"
B 2" × 6"
C 1½" × 6"
D 3" Circle (template 4)

season's greetings

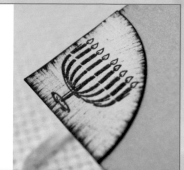

For the pattern to Three Tiers (left) see page 66.

For the pattern to Well Rounded (top right) see page 27.

For the pattern to Left Eclipse (bottom right) see page 64.

THREE WISHES ™

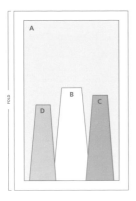

4¾" × 3"

paper dimensions

A	4½" × 2¾"
B	2½" × 1"
C	2¼" × 1"
D	2" × 1"

instructions

1 Using the Three Wishes templates provided, trim pieces B, C, and D.

2 Using a 4¾" × 3" card, with the fold on the left side as your base, attach piece A to the center of the card front.

3 Attach piece B, C, and D to the bottom of piece A with the tops spaced evenly and the bottoms overlapping.

4 Embellish as desired.

ideas! *For more artwork featuring this pattern see page 48.*

NOTEWORTHY ™

4¾" × 3"

paper dimensions

A	3" × 2½"
B	1¾" × 2¼"
C	2" × 2½"

instructions

1 Using a 4¾" × 3" card with the fold on the left side as your base, attach piece A to the card front, placing it ¼" from the top, keeping the side edges flush.

2 Attach piece B to the center of piece C.

3 Attach piece C to the card front, placing it 1" from the top and centered from side to side.

4 Embellish as desired.

ideas! *For more artwork featuring this pattern see page 16.*

season's greetings

For holiday time or anytime you need to make a bold statement, you'll love our Greetings Card Workshop. This extraordinarily paper-thrifty project will help you make 16 standard 5½" × 4¼" cards (two each of eight designs) using just three sheets of paper, plus card bases. So much fun and such a great value, too! To get started, gather the following materials:

12" × 12" cardstock (2)
12" × 12" Background and Texture paper (1)
5½" × 4¼" card bases (16)

For this card workshop, you can use pre-cut standard card bases, or easily make your own. To make your own card bases, you'll need 10 sheets of 8½" × 11" cardstock in colors that coordinate with your accent cardstocks and Background and Texture papers. Cut each sheet of 8½" × 11" cardstock in half (width-wise), score at the center of each cut piece and fold. Voilà! A perfect card base in seconds. For best results, choose dramatic contrasts between your card bases, cardstock, and patterned paper—this will provide visual interest even for

this very economical project. Next, follow the cutting diagrams and assembly instructions to put your cards together. Keep it affordable by stamping your embellishments instead of using consumable accents—here, the stars shine and the sentiments pop, keeping everything merry and bright, for just pennies per card.

CARDSTOCK

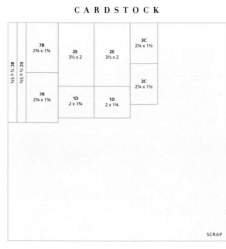

CARDSTOCK

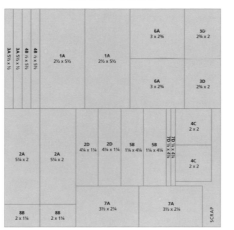

B & T PAPER

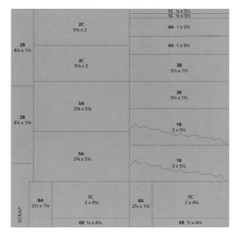

C A R D   1

instructions

1 Using a 4¼" × 5½" card with the fold on the top as your base, attach piece 1A to the top of the card front, keeping the edges flush.

2 Attach piece 1B to the top of the card front, keeping the edges flush.

3 Attach piece 1C to piece 1A, placing it ⅛" from the bottom, keeping the side edges flush.

4 Attach piece 1D to the card front, placing it 1½" from the top and ½" from the left edge.

5 Embellish as desired.

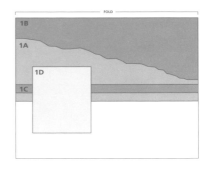

4¼" × 5½"

paper dimensions

1A 2½" × 5½"
1B 2" × 5½" (torn)
1C ¼" × 5½"
1D 2" × 1¾"

C A R D   2

instructions

1 Using a 5½" × 4¼" card with the fold on the left as your base, attach piece 2A to the card front, placing it ⅛" from the top and left edges.

2 Attach piece 2B to piece 2A, placing it ½" from the top, keeping the right edges flush.

3 Attach piece 2C to the card front, placing it ⅛" from the top and right edges.

4 Attach piece 2D to piece 2C, placing it ½" from the top, keeping the left edges flush.

5 Attach piece 2E to the center of the card front.

6 Embellish as desired.

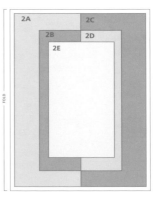

5½" × 4¼"

paper dimensions

2A 5¼" × 2"
2B 4¼" × 1¼"
2C 5¼" × 2"
2D 4¼" × 1¼"
2E 3½" × 2"

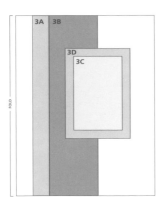

$5^{1}/_{2}$" × $4^{1}/_{4}$"

paper dimensions

3A $5^{1}/_{2}$" × $^{1}/_{2}$"
3B $5^{1}/_{2}$" × $1^{1}/_{2}$"
3C $2^{1}/_{4}$" × $1^{1}/_{2}$"
3D $2^{3}/_{4}$" × 2"

instructions

1 Using a $5^{1}/_{2}$" × $4^{1}/_{4}$" card with the fold on the left side as your base, attach piece 3A to the card front, placing it $^{1}/_{2}$" from the left edge, keeping the top and bottom flush.

2 Attach piece 3B directly to the right of piece 3A, keeping the edges flush.

3 Attach piece 3C to the center of piece 3D.

4 Attach piece 3D to the card front, placing it 1" from the top and $1^{1}/_{2}$" from the left edge.

5 Embellish as desired.

$4^{1}/_{4}$" × $5^{1}/_{2}$"

paper dimensions

4A 1" × $5^{1}/_{2}$"
4B $^{1}/_{2}$" × $5^{1}/_{2}$"
4C 2" × 2"

instructions

1 Using a $4^{1}/_{4}$" × $5^{1}/_{2}$" card with the fold on the top as your base, attach piece 4A to the card front, placing it $^{3}/_{4}$" from the bottom, keeping the side edges flush.

2 Attach piece 4B directly above piece 4A, keeping the edges flush.

3 Attach piece 4C to the card front, placing it $^{3}/_{4}$" from the top and 1" from the right edge.

4 Embellish as desired.

card workshop

season's greetings

card workshop

CARD 5

instructions

1 Using a 4¼" × 5½" card with the fold on the top as your base, attach piece 5A to the card front, placing it ⅛" from the bottom and centered from side to side.

2 Attach piece 5B to the card front, placing it 1" from the top and centered from side to side.

3 Embellish as desired.

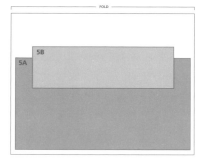

4¼" × 5½"

paper dimensions

5A 2¾" × 5¼"
5B 1¼" × 4¼"

CARD 6

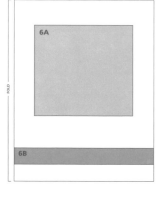

instructions

1 Using a 5½" × 4¼" card with the fold on the left side as your base, attach piece 6A to the card front, placing it ¾" from the top and centered from side to side.

2 Attach piece 6B to the card front, placing it ½" from the bottom, keeping the side edges flush.

3 Embellish as desired.

5½" × 4¼"

paper dimensions

6A 3" × 2¾"
6B ½" × 4¼"

5½" × 4¼"

paper dimensions

7A 3½" × 2¼"
7B 2¾" × 1¾"
7C 2" × 4¼"
7D ¼" × 4¼"

instructions

1 Using a 5½" × 4¼" card with the fold on the left side as your base, attach piece 7A to the top left side, keeping the edges flush.

2 Attach piece 7B to the center of piece 7A.

3 Attach piece 7C to the bottom of the card front, keeping the edges flush.

4 Attach piece 7D to piece 7C ½" from the bottom, keeping the side edges flush.

5 Embellish as desired.

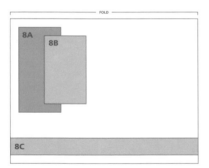

4¼" × 5½"

paper dimensions

8A 2½" × 1¼"
8B 2" × 1¼"
8C ½" × 5½"

instructions

1 Using a 5½" x 4¼" card with the fold on the left side as your base, attach piece 8A to the card front, placing it ¼" from the top and left edge.

2 Attach piece 8B to the card front, placing it ½" from the top and 1" from the left edge.

3 Attach piece 8C to the card front, placing it ¼" from the bottom, keeping the side edges flush.

4 Embellish as desired.

waiting

4

YOU

For the pattern to
Medallion see page 52.

For the pattern to Lucky Layers
(right) see page 27.

C E N T E R   C I R C L E S ™

instructions

1 Using a 4½" circle card (template 1) with the fold on the top as your base, attach pieces A, B, and C to the center of the card front as desired to form a cluster.

2 Embellish as desired.

paper dimensions

A 2½" Circle (template 5)
B 2" Circle (template 6)
C 1½" Circle (template 7)

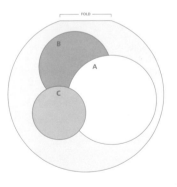

FOLD

4½" CIRCLE

ideas! *For more artwork featuring this pattern see page 55.*

Jeanette's Tip

Add a handwritten sentiment over painted journaling lines for a trendy twist.

YOU MAY BE OUT OF *my sight,*
BUT NEVER OUT OF *my mind.*
THINKING *of you!*

TIPS & TECHNIQUES
puddle pad

step 1 Place several dots of multiple colors of re-inker on a piece of felt. (Make sure to place an absorbent layer under the felt.)

step 2 Press stamp into felt pad and stamp image onto cardstock.

paper dimensions

A 5" × 2½"
B 1½" × 3"
C 8½" × 3½"

instructions

1 Using the Sentiment Wave template provided, trim piece C.

2 Using an 8" × 3½" card with the fold on the left side as your base, attach piece A to the top right corner of the card front, keeping the edges flush.

3 Attach piece B to the card front, placing it 2" from the bottom, keeping the left edges flush.

4 Attach piece C to the right side of the card front, keeping the straight edges flush.

5 Embellish as desired.

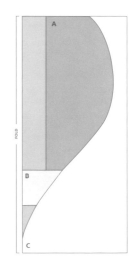

8" × 3½"

ideas! *For more artwork featuring this pattern see page 32.*

thinking of you

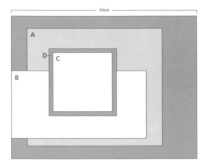

4¼" × 5½"

paper dimensions

A 3½" × 4"
B 2" × 4"
C 1¾" × 1¾"
D 2¼" × 2¼"

instructions

1 Using a 4¼" × 5½" card with the fold on the top as your base, attach piece A to the card front, placing it ⅜" from the top and left edge.

2 Attach piece B to the card front, placing it 1 ⅝" from the top, keeping the left edges flush.

3 Attach piece C to the center of piece D.

4 Attach piece D to the card front, placing it 1" from the top and left edges.

5 Embellish as desired

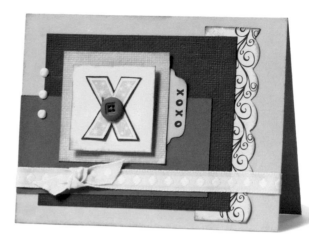

ideas! *For more artwork featuring this pattern see page 48.*

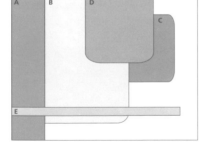

4¼" × 5½"

paper dimensions

A 4¼" × 1"
B 3¾" × 2½"
C 2" × 1½"
D 2" × 2¼"
E ¼" × 5"

instructions

1 Using a 4¼" × 5½" card with the fold on the top as your base, attach piece A to the left side of the card front, keeping the edges flush.

2 Attach piece B to the card front, placing it directly to the right of piece A, keeping the top flush.

3 Attach piece C to the card front, placing it directly to the right of piece B, ½" from the top.

4 Attach piece D to the card front, placing it 2¼" from the left side, keeping the top flush.

5 Attach piece E to the card front, placing it ¾" from the bottom, keeping the left edge flush.

6 Embellish as desired.

ideas! *For more artwork featuring this pattern see page 58.*

thinking of you

Jeanette's Tip

Make the inside of your card as beautiful as the front by adding dimension to focal images.

Treasure Life's Little Moments

Life is nothing without

For the pattern to Down the Middle
(left) see page 35.
For the pattern to Framework
(right) see page 15.

4½" × 4½"

paper dimensions

A   4¼" × 2¾"
B   4¼" × 1½"
C   1" × 2¾"
D   2" × 2"

ideas! *For more artwork featuring this pattern see page 91.*

instructions

1   Using the Up in the Corner template provided, trim piece D.

2   Using a 4½" × 4½" card with the fold on the top as your base, attach piece A to the card front, placing it ⅛" from the top and right edge.

3   Attach piece B to the card front, placing it ⅛" from the top and left edge.

4   Attach piece C to the card front, placing it ½" from the top and ¼" from the right edge.

5   Attach piece D to the card front, placing it ⅛" from the top and left edges.

6   Embellish as desired.

W I N D O W   W I S H E S ™

4½" × 4½"

paper dimensions

A   2½" × 2½"
B   2½" × 2½"

ideas! *For more artwork featuring this pattern see page 91.*

instructions

1   Using a 4½" × 4½" card with the fold on the top as your base, cut a 2" × 2" square out of the card front, ½" from the top and right edge.

2   Attach piece A to the inside of the card back, placing it ¼" from the top and right edges.

3   Cut a 2" × 2" square from the center of piece B. Attach piece B to the card front, framing the 2 × 2" cutout.

4   Embellish as desired.

thinking of you

thinking of you

TIPS & TECHNIQUES
rock 'n roll

step 1 Ink your stamp with a base color. Stamp image onto cardstock.

step 2 After cleaning the stamp, roll the edges in a darker color, being careful to ink only the outer edges. Align the stamp over the base color image and stamp.

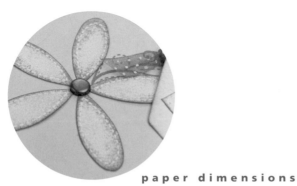

instructions

1 Using the Confidential templates provided, trim pieces A and D.

2 Using piece A with the fold on the left side as your base, attach piece B to the center of the card front, keeping the left edges flush.

3 Attach piece C to piece B, ¼" from the bottom and centered from side to side, adhering only the bottom and side edges in order to form a pocket.

4 Insert piece D into the pocket formed by piece C.

5 Attach pieces E to the sides of pieces F, forming tabs.

6 Insert pieces F into the card.

7 Embellish as desired.

paper dimensions

A 9¾" × 7"
B 6¼" × 4½"
C 2¼" × 4"
D 3¼" × 2"
E 1½" Circle (template 7) (4)
F 6" × 4½" (4) (not shown in blueprint)

7" × 5"

ideas! *For more artwork featuring this pattern see page 74.*

CORNER SHOP™

For the pattern to this card see page 39.

MATCHBOOK™

For the pattern to this card see page 76.

INNER COURT™

For the pattern to this card see page 67.

SIMPLY SECURE™

For the pattern to this card see page 46.

thinking of you

For the pattern to Small Wonder
(left) see page 101.

Jeanette's Tip

Perfectly color in any stamped line image by using watercolor pencils and a blending pen.

· · · · GEOMETRIC ™ · · · ·

instructions

1 Using a 5½" × 4¼" card with the fold on the left side as your base, attach piece A to the card front placing it ½" from the right edge, keeping the top flush.

2 Attach piece B to piece A, placing it ½" from the top and centered from side to side.

3 Attach piece C to the center of piece B.

4 Embellish as desired.

paper dimensions

A 4" × 3"

B 2¼" × 2¼"

C 2" Circle (template 6)

5½" × 4¼"

ideas! *For more artwork featuring this pattern see page 48.*

WHEN WE'RE *together* OR WHEN WE'RE APART,
YOU'RE FIRST IN MY *thoughts*
AND FIRST IN MY *heart.*

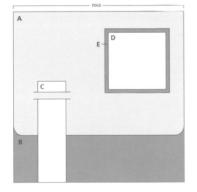

6" × 6"

ideas! *For more artwork featuring this pattern see page 60.*

instructions

1 Using the Designer Tab template provided, fold and cut slits in piece A to create a 6" × 6" card with the fold on the top.

2 Attach piece B to the bottom of the inside card back, keeping the edges flush.

3 Attach piece C to the card back, 1" from the left side, fold over to the card front and slide through slits.

4 Attach piece D to the center of piece E.

5 Attach piece E to the card front, placing it ¾" from the top and right edge.

6 Embellish as desired.

TIPS & TECHNIQUES
stamping with markers

step 1 Using colored markers, add multiple colors to your stamp.

step 2 Breathe on the stamp or spritz with a fine mist to moisten ink. Stamp image on cardstock.

paper dimensions

A	10½" × 6"
B	2" × 6"
C	4" × 1"
D	2" × 2"
E	2¼" × 2¼"

thinking of you

Jeanette's Tip

Spice up the inside of your card by decorating it with images and embellishments in addition to your sentiment.

WISHING YOU WELL

grateful hearts

For the pattern to Fancy File
(left) see page 81.
For the pattern to Middle Ground
(right) see page 19.

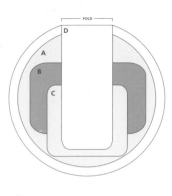

4½" CIRCLE

paper dimensions

A   4" Circle (template 2)
B   2" × 3¼"
C   2" × 2¼"
D   1½" × 3¾"

ideas! *For more artwork featuring this pattern see page 63.*

instructions

1   Using a 4½" circle card (template 1) with the fold on the top as your base, attach piece A to the center of the card front.

2   Attach piece B to the card front, placing it 1" from the top and centered from side to side.

3   Attach piece C to the card front, placing it ½" from the bottom and centered from side to side.

4   Attach piece D to the card front keeping the top flush and centered from side to side.

5   Embellish as desired.

4½" CIRCLE

paper dimensions

A   ¾" × 4"
B   2" × 2"
C   2⅛" × 2⅛"
D   1½" Circle (template 7)

ideas! *For more artwork featuring this pattern see page 65.*

instructions

1   Using a 4½" circle card (template 1) with the fold on the left side as your base, attach piece A to the card front, placing it ½" from the top. Trim edges.

2   Attach piece B to the center of piece C.

3   Attach piece C to the card front, placing it ¾" from the bottom and ¾" left edge.

4   Attach piece D to the bottom right corner of pieces B and C.

5   Embellish as desired.

index